I0791340

HOW TO DESTROY AMERICA

SAMUEL CHEN

Archway Publishing books may be ordered through booksellers or by contacting:

Archway Publishing
1663 Liberty Drive
Bloomington, IN 47403
www.archwaypublishing.com
844-669-3957

ISBN: 978-1-6657-1989-6 (sc)
ISBN: 978-1-6657-1988-9 (hc)
ISBN: 978-1-6657-1990-2 (e)

Library of Congress Control Number: 2022903962

Print information available on the last page.

Archway Publishing rev. date: 4/29/2022

Contents

Publications

2011   *Glance to the World*, *In the Beginning*, and *Butch Letters of Yangon*, three books of essays

2012   *The Grace*, *Traveling to Hong Kong* (a travelogue), and *The Thorn Crown*, three books of essays

2013   *Patience*, and *A Series of Stories of Lushan*, two books of essays

2014   *Refugee Stories of Syria*, and *My Superstar*, two books of essays

2015   *Escaping Chronicle*, a novel, and *Escaping Course*, an essay

2016   *Escaping Stories*, essays, and *Some Love Letters on the Escaping Way*, a novel

2017   *Escape Enlightenment*, essays; *A Chinese Refugee and His American Lovers*, a novel; and *Assassination Tutorial*, a manual

2018   *Dodging Ghosts*, anthology

2019   *Rainbow Will Rise Up*, anthology

To the Global Dictators

Dear global dictators, hello.

In the past one hundred years, it has not been easy to maintain dictatorship because the United States has assumed for itself the role of the world's police, and it was necessary to maintain law, order, and civilization on the earth and not to allow too many authoritarian regimes to survive.

Nowadays, that's good news. The president of the United States at the time of this writing, Mr. Donald Trump, decided not to make the United States the global police. He began to shrink the circle of war and the influence of the United States from the world stage. He planned only to manage the United States well. However, he was and is wrong.

This is an era of the internet.

This is a global village.

This is a whole new world.

The lifestyle of all mankind is interconnected and inseparable. How can it be cut apart? A butterfly in Africa flapping its wings will produce the butterfly effect, causing the United States to collapse. President Trump's shortsightedness, arbitrariness, and arrogance will have inevitably led the United States to decline.

How can a policeman partner with a group of thieves in a community? What would happen if he chose to do this? The security of the entire community would become chaotic, horrible, and dangerous. This would be a disaster.

How can the richest gentleman do business with a group of the most despicable thieves in a town? What would happen if he chose to do this? The richest gentleman would be killed, his property stolen, and his wife and daughters raped and turned into sex slaves. This would also be a disaster.

Today, the United States and many rogue countries have become close friends. So what are you waiting for?

Dear global dictators, you should unite and move in unison to further the decline of the United States, pushing the United States to perish.

How to send the United States into extinction? The way is to let the United States disintegrate and the states declare independence, as the United States has become a confederate country like Europe. The divided United States will no longer be a powerful military country but simply a union of many small countries. In this way, it can no longer manage international affairs. In these circumstances, you can do whatever you want.

Dear global dictators, after the demise of the United States, you can quickly push the giant wheel of history and move all humankind to the dark abyss that will never end. You can restore the monarchy, passing it on from generation to generation, and make it into hereditary succession, keeping your people as slaves to support you.

This book proposes how to destroy the United States. Please read it carefully and put it into practice.

May your dynasties flourish forever in eternal prosperity.

March 13, 2020
Washington, DC

Author Photo

(March 7, 2019, Washington, DC)

Preface

Dear friends, hello.

As I write, it is June 19, 2020. In November of this year, the United States will hold an election. It will be five months before we can know who the next US president will be.

However, in my anthology *Rainbow Will Rise Up* (2019), I insulted the current US president, Donald Trump, as a political she-male. In this year's anthology *How to Destroy America*, I am cursing him as a shit-eating emperor. I am translating both these books into English for publication in the United States. So what will happen if President Donald Trump is reelected?

If he loses this year, I will live in the United States very safely. If he is reelected, I will be persecuted, forced to sneak away and flee from the United States.

If he is reelected, he will become a dictator, and the United States will become a dictatorship. Dictatorships are refugee-exporting countries. If Trump is reelected, the United States will produce a large number of political refugees, and everyone will scramble to flee the United States.

If he is reelected this year, the United States will perish in the next fifty years. So I put forth this book as a historical witness, so that everyone might verify my prediction.

If he is reelected, the world will enter the polar-night era in the next thousand years, and humankind will lose all hope of a better future.

The world is so sad. But if this is God's arrangement, is it still necessary? God wants to test the loyalty of humankind and arranges for a lot of devils and sufferings to appear. In the midst of trouble, we can only maintain faith, hope, love, and joy.

And I, as a writer, in order to promote the great progress of history, can only write this book and publish it, leaving a proof of my times. In my times, I have worked hard and fought for the happiness of all humankind.

May the Lord bless everyone.

June 19, 2020
Washington, DC

1

Let Us Save Hong Kong Together!

Mr. Liang:

Have you decided to make Guangdong an independent country?

Have you decided to use kapok as the national flower of Guangdong?

Have you decided to use the song "Kapok," by the Hong Kong singer Mr. Rowan, as the national anthem?

Have you decided to designate the nation of Guangdong as the Republic of Guangdong?

Have you decided to design and make the national flag of Guangdong?

If you have decided, I will work for you.

Next year, I will be able to make an appeal for the national establishment of Guangdong's independence in the White House.

Next year, I will sing the song "Kapok" while holding a guitar in the White House.

Once you decide, I will gladly go for you.

The preceding is a letter I wrote to Mr. Liang, who is a member of the Democratic Party of China. He is a subordinate to Mr. Wang Juntao and is a Cantonese.

I have exchanged my views with him about Guangdong's need to move toward independence and nationhood. In fact, everything is urgent! Hong Kong's Anti-Extradition Law Amendment Bill Movement must be quickly suppressed by the Chinese Communist Party (CCP). In order to ensure the success of Hong Kong's anti-amendment campaign, the Guangdong Independence Movement must be launched immediately!

In the future, as long as Guangdong is independent, then Guangdong can form an effective geographic barrier to permanently block the Yankees' southward invasion and completely protect the tranquility of Hong Kong.

At present, how to quickly suppress the anti-amendment campaign in Hong Kong? Chinese emperor Xi Jinping has already convened a Hong Kong conference on suppressing counterrevolution in Zhongnanhai. The consensus at the conference has been that an assassination agency must be quickly formed, similar to the Soviet Union's Cheka, and similar to the antirevolutionary committee in the early years of the founding of China, allowing it to carry out assassination operations in Hong Kong to kill Hong Kong's brave factions.

Some time ago, in order to intimidate the brave factions of Hong Kong, the Hong Kong "black police" captured some beautiful Hong Kong girls, took them back to the police stations for gang rape, and then threw them into the sea to feed the fish. However, after the Hong Kong Anti-Revolutionary Conference convened, the new action resolution has been to arrest all the brave factions, then destroy the corpses and leave no traces of them on the earth.

Since then, no beautiful Hong Kong girls have been thrown

into the sea to feed the fish. Instead, they are transformed into light smoke, rise into floating clouds, and disappear in silence.

Now that Xi Jinping is going to kill the brave factions of Hong Kong, we should be with those martyrs and turn ourselves into light smoke spread into the clouds. I call upon my fellow Cantonese to take part in the Guangdong Independence Movement and accompany the martyrs of Hong Kong in dying together. This is what morality demands!

Dear founders of the provinces of China, let us go on to establish these independent countries together. It is the only way to save Hong Kong. When the heroes of all provinces of this country show their independent will, the total number of assassinations of the Hong Kong brave factions will decrease.

Dear founding fathers of all provinces, let us compel Xi Jinping to add congestion, chaos, and troubles. As long as he wants to kill the brave factions of Hong Kong, we will put our own lives on and let him kill us!

This is the most sophisticated means of political strategy. Xi Jinping wants to kill the brave factions of Hong Kong, and we simply declare the independence of the provinces in the United States. In this way, we can entice the assassination force of the Chinese Ministry of National Security to carry out assassination activities in the United States. As soon as Xi Jinping launches a large-scale assassination in the United States, it will trigger the resentment and resistance of the CIA and the FBI. He did so deceivingly—to bully Americans!

In this way, the next president of the United States will listen to the opinions of the staff and kill Xi Jinping.

As soon as the US president makes some adjustments to his China policy, Xi Jinping will definitely die.

Last time, when Mr. Ilshat H. Kkbore, Mr. He Anquan, and Mr. Wang Qingying held an independent movement meeting in the US Congress, some founding fathers actually used their objects to cover their faces, fearing that they would be assassinated by CCP agents. This is very embarrassing. If you are afraid of death, don't be a founding father. What's the point of you not taking shit in the latrine?

So, dear Cantonese, if you don't want to die, just recommend me to be the founding father of Guangdong!

I am happy to die in order to save the brave factions of Hong Kong. Please don't take away my rights to die.

October 22, 2019
Washington, DC

2

I Am a Great Man!

I am really a great man.

Before I was born, all the Chinese fled to the United States for some two hundred years. They are self-proclaimed as slaves and as second-class citizens and will never admit that they are the masters of the United States.

They are always whispering, swallowing, timid as mice, for fear of being sent back to China by the US government.

But now, I was born and arrived in the United States. I sweep the distress of the Chinese people for the two hundred years. I, as a refugee, have decided to kick US President Donald Trump out of the White House.

Only because of my appearance in the United States will the Chinese people be proud and full being comfortable.

Unfortunately, my actions were blocked last year. An elder of the Federation for a Democratic China asked me to endure and wait. Then, the event has been dragging on for a year. Next year, in 2020, I expect President Donald Trump to continue to win his reelection. That is better. During his tenure, I have enough time to march and kicked him out of the White House.

I have made a great contribution to the Chinese. How

should the Chinese repay me? - The Chinese are really beasts, not people, with no conscience. The Chinese should give me a bronze statue and a monument. But now, the Chinese are only digging a deep pit for me and want to kill me with stones and bury me.

I am the greatest man who has contributed to the Chinese in the last two hundred years. However, the Chinese have no conscience. The Chinese nation does not have a good person. This nation should be ruined.

November 2, 2019
Washington, DC

3

How to Complete the Total Massacre in Hong Kong

Dear fools, I am a great scientist and the founder of Principles of Suicide. In my Principles of Suicide, which I founded in 2002, I have explained the academic concept of the suicide constant to everyone.

What is the suicide constant? —— Every city and every country has a constant for annual suicide rate. If the operating background of political, economic, cultural, religious, scientific, and other factors does not change, the suicide constant will not change accordingly.

The suicide rate in Hong Kong was that before 1997, for every 40,000 Hong Kong people, 1 person committed suicide.

The suicide constant in China was that in 1999, for every 100,000 Chinese, 28 people committed suicide.

This shows that the suicide rate in China is more than 10 times higher than that in Hong Kong.

At present, the suicide rate in China continues to rise, becoming the highest in the world. In my Assassination Tutorial, which I wrote in 2017, this is laid out very clearly. Now, 350,000 Chinese commit suicide every year. Thus, by finding 3,500 suicides to assassinate the corrupt Chinese officials, China's democracy can basically be realized.

Dear fools, what is the importance of analyzing these suicide data? —— What I need to focus on is the situation in Hong Kong. The suicide rate in Hong Kong was one suicide for every 40,000 people. In other words, Hong Kong currently has a population of 8 million, and at most 200 people commit suicide every year.

However, obviously, this year's data has begun to change. Recently, the director of Hong Kong's Security Bureau, Mr. Li Jiachao, responded in writing to Mr. Xu Zhifeng, a member of Hong Kong's Legislative Council: Since the Anti-Amendment Campaign, in just a few months, the Hong Kong policemen have killed 3,000 Hong Kong citizens, and Hong Kong citizens have killed zero Hong Kong policemen.

Regarding Mr. Li Jiachao's report, Radio Free Asia has a detailed report. Let me give you an appendix.

Dear fools, however, comparing with the June 4 Massacre in 1989, Mr. Li Jiachao's report is indeed not illusory enough. Or Mr. Li Jiachao doesn't want to be called a liar.

After the June 4 Massacre broke out in 1989, Chinese State Council spokesperson Mr. Yuan Mu said: "No one died in Tiananmen Square." Later, Mr. Yuan Mu was honored as a liar. But this time, Mr. Li Jiachao, the director of the Security Bureau of Hong Kong, actually said: "Hong Kong police killed 3,000 Hong Kong citizens." It seems that Mr. Li Jiachao does not want to be called a liar.

However, judging from the figures reported by Mr. Li Jiachao, it seems that there are still a few hundred Hong Kong corpses to make up 3,000 people. —— Yes. However, Hong

Kong is currently an assassination city, and its statistics must be inaccurate because of:

First, the relatives of some demonstrators are not around at all; they may be in foreign countries. The martyrs died, and no one called the police.

Second, after some demonstrators died, their relatives were discouraged and too lazy to call the police and sent them directly to the funeral home.

Third, after some people called the police, the police did not agree to investigate because all the personnel at the stations had been sent to the streets to suppress the demonstrators, and no one got involved in the investigation.

Fourth, even if the police accepted the cases, the police stations did not bother to report and summarize. Everyone was in a state of sabotage during the turmoil.

Fifth, even if the police do report and summarize, the data sent to the director of the Security Bureau in Hong Kong may be missed. And there are no statistics, because the officers have seen too many dead people and cannot be bothered to care about how many people have died.

Dear fools, now, we scientists, in the field of political science, have to make forward-looking research reports. So how many people does the CCP intend to massacre in Hong Kong during the Anti-Amendment Campaign? —— It is estimated that more than 40,000 Hong Kong people will be killed.

The last time, in the June 4 Massacre in 1989, the CCP massacred more than 30,000 Chinese in Beijing. This is according to the very detailed research report recently made by Japanese scholars. Every deceased, name, age, and identity, that no one is missing and there is a case can for investigation. So this time, in the Anti-Amendment Campaign in 2019, if the CCP killed more than 40,000 people in Hong Kong, that would also be the normal scope of work and the inertia of action.

So, how is the total massacre of more than 40,000 calculated? —— In 1950, Chairman Mao Zedong decided to carry out the Anti-Rebellion Campaign, killing people according to one-thousandth of the population. Later, the campaign was expanded, and some areas killed 20 per thousand people. But on the whole, China had completed the Anti-Rebellion Campaign at a rate of five per thousand. So, this time, Chairman Xi Jinping wants to learn from Chairman Mao Zedong, and of course he will promote the Anti-Rebellion Campaign in Hong Kong. Then, it will be imperative to set up an assassination bureau to host the assassination business in Hong Kong.

Hong Kong has a population of 8 million. If one in a thousand people should be killed, 8,000 Hong Kong people will be killed. So far, 3,000 have been killed, which leaves 5,000 people still to be killed.

However, history always repeats. The Cultural Revolution is repeated, the monarchy is repeated, and the suppression of rebellion will be repeated. The Anti-Rebellion Campaign in Hong Kong will of course be expanded, and history will always repeat itself. Then, according to the ratio of five thousandths, more than 40,000 Hong Kong people must be killed.

However, history will not simply repeat. In the past, Chairman Mao Zedong ordered the police to enter people's homes to have them arrested or simply shot to death. But now, Hong Kong police cannot enter homes casually to kill people. Then, the assassination job undertaken by the Hong Kong Assassination Bureau will be very onerous. It is not easy to assassinate the targets one by one when killing more than 40,000 people. It must take at least two years to complete, killing more than 20,000 people every year.

However, assassinating 2,000 Hong Kong people every month is not an easy workload. Therefore, the assassination and the public killing must be combined at the same time. Send troops, and blatantly kill a group first. Then send secret police to kill another group secretly. This method is the best.

Well, let's continue to observe and research. We must trust the Chinese Communist Party. They must have the ability and means to complete the total massacre of 40,000 corpses.

11/17/2019
Washington, DC

4

I Am the Presiding Dog-Trainer of the World!

The night before yesterday, I brought Mr. Wang Kaiming and another friend to the home of Mr. Wei Jingsheng, the godfather of the Chinese democracy movement, for dinner.

During the dinner, Mr. Wei Jingsheng suddenly said something like this: "The nephew of the former US Secretary of Defense, Mr. Mattis, is a good friend of mine. He often asks me about China affairs. He is now an assistant to the US Senator, Mr. Rubio."

I was taken aback when I heard it. The distinctive personality of the former Secretary of Defense of the United States I much admired. He has a clear love and hatred, and courage and perseverance. Unfortunately, a clever man cannot get along with an old idiot. He is such a good general but had been still fired by President Trump.

I sighed: "What a pity! President Trump fired him and replaced him with an idiot as Secretary of Defense."

When Mr. Wei Jingsheng heard me cursing the US Secretary of Defense, Mr. Patrick Shanahan, as an idiot, he immediately laughed and nodded and said: "He was a boss of an arms company before he became the Secretary of Defense."

Why can I judge that Secretary of Defense Patrick Shanahan is a fool? This judgment reflects my top political science. Because Patrick Shanahan's words and deeds violated the quotations from Dr. Wang Juntao.

Quotations from Dr. Wang Juntao represent the highest state of contemporary political science.

Did Patrick Shanahan behave inappropriately? After he became the Secretary of Defense of the United States, he offered this stupid saying: "The US military is the most powerful in the world and can destroy its opponents anywhere on the earth." —— Such stupid statements can only be made by fools, because the United States is a strong man but infected with an ideological virus, lying ill in bed, and any weak sclerotic ghost can perch on his bedside to kill him.

The US military power is completely meaningless. A dying, unconscious patient, no matter how powerful, will only die in the torment of the disease, alas!

This summer, one day I had breakfast with Dr. Wang Juntao, chairman of the Democratic Party of China who deserved a PhD in political science from Columbia University. He told me this: "In order for China to buy 2 million tons of American soybeans, President Trump decided to treat 11 US aircraft carrier battle groups as scrap iron." —— This is one of the quotations of Dr. Wang Juntao. It has answered one of the most cutting-edge phenomena in contemporary politics: penetration.

In other words, China's ideological infiltration power can completely defeat the most sophisticated US military power.

Those who admire American military power, including the

world's democracy fighters, including US Secretary of Defense Patrick Shanahan, are fools!

China can completely defeat the United States through infiltration methods, especially the infiltration of forces.

At present, China's penetration has reached such a level that the best friend of President Trump's favorite daughter Ivanka is a Chinese spy.

At present, the highest level of China's penetration is this: US President Trump has become a vicious dog at the feet of Chinese Emperor Xi Jinping. He tells it to bite whoever it bites.

Xi Jinping asked Trump to kill the Chinese people. Trump immediately killed Xinjiang people and Hong Kong people.

Xi Jinping asked Trump to kill the American people. Trump immediately went crazy in the United States, arguing with the US House of Representatives and Senate, and arguing with the media and newspapers all over the United States.

So if Trump is reelected in 2020, will the United States perish under the infiltration of China? —— Even if it does not die, only half of its life remains. The United States will definitely be dying thanks to Trump's craziness, and its vitality will be greatly injured.

Okay, do you understand? Now that President Trump has become a vicious dog fed by Xi Jinping, the combat mission of the overseas democracy movement must be revised. I changed the general program of the overseas democracy movement from a dog-worshiping activity to a dog-training game.

Dogs are for taming, not for bowing. Dear pro-democracy leaders, are you ready to kneel down to a dog? Do you want to worship a dog? This is wrong.

Everyone should tie a dog collar around the dog's neck, and then take the leash to play dog-training games.

Do you understand? Since then, the task of the overseas democracy movement is to train dogs and practice kung fu for a dog.

And I am the presiding dog-trainer of the world. Because I foresaw that, I decided to go to the White House to raise the inflatable dolls and start a dog-training game a year ago. Now, I am translating *Rainbow Will Rise Up* to publish; it is also useful for training the dog.

Currently, I arrive at the White House every Sunday to build the Lennon Wall for training the dog. The dog-training game—who can play it earlier, braver, with more determination and perseverance than I?

I am the presiding dog-trainer of the world!

November 27, 2019
Washington, DC

5

The Battle Is Over!

This long war of the Chinese democracy movement is actually over! The Chinese people have won, and China is about to gain democracy! If we continue this battle, we are actually just pretending to be forced. There is no need.

The battle is over because the US Congress has passed the Magnitsky Act, the Hong Kong Bill of Rights, and the Uyghur Bill of Rights. The three major bills all point to an established political goal: to freeze the property of Chinese emperor Xi Jinping.

As long as the US government orders the freezing of Xi Jinping's assets, it will inevitably announce the scale of Xi Jinping's overseas assets. What will happen to the Chinese people when they hear that Xi Jinping has a trillion US dollars in assets abroad? Then none of Xi Jinping's anticorruption actions can any longer be carried out. Those high-ranking Chinese officials who have been restless under the butcher knife will have to take coup measures in order to get revenge.

The battle is over! In the future, the only effective work we can do is to let the US government freeze Xi Jinping's property. So who will be responsible for lobbying the White House? The current prodemocracy leaders in the area of Washington, DC, shake their heads and refuse to agree. They will never lobby the White House. They believe that after China has achieved democracy, all the prodemocracy leaders will be unemployed, and all the prodemocracy movement teams will be disbanded. Then how can we live again? Life is an illusion and too much change to adapt to.

I can tell everyone a real secret. You constantly say that, if one day the prodemocracy leaders come to power, they will be worse than the Communist Party. This proves that you are the fools!

The overseas prodemocracy leaders are not stupid. None of them will return to their country to take power. They already know that after China has achieved democracy, there will be decades of turmoil. They are too old to suffer for decades. In the next ten years, they only want to retire in the United States, and then they will buy coffins, choose their graves, and bury themselves in the United States. In other words, in essence, China's democracy movement has not done business with any great leader of the Chinese democratic movement.

The battle is over! At present, as long as any major leader of the Chinese democracy movement moves from the suburban to settle in the area of Washington, DC, China will immediately realize democracy. So who can move in and settle in Washington, DC? I can only pin my hopes on Ms. Jin Xiuhong and Mr. Xiong Yan.

Ms. Jin Xiuhong is chairwoman of the United States branch of the Federation for a Democratic China (FDC). Some time ago, she visited Washington, DC, and Mr. Zhao Yan strongly advocated that she should move into that area and settle down. I am convinced that if she is willing to move, then she can go to the White House to lobby. She alone can overthrow the Communist Party.

Xiong Yan, the leader of the 8964 student movement, is an army chaplain in the United States. He is about to run for the House of Representatives. If he can be elected, of course he will move to Washington, DC to settle down. Then I will devise a political conspiracy to instigate 535 members of the US Congress to lobby in the White House. He can overthrow the Communist Party by himself.

The battle is over! The work of the overseas democratic movement continues to be forced year after year and remains unchanged. It has been advanced for thirty years in the past, and it will be for another thirty years. However, there is really no need to pretend. As long as someone goes to the White House to lobby, the battle is over. In the years to come, everyone can pretend that just to entertain themselves, nothing needs to be serious.

Many philanthropists said: "I haven't donated enough money to the prodemocracy tycoons; how can China achieve democracy?" This remark evinces delusion.

Many pro-democracy leaders said: "I have not yet established a rigorous opposition party; how can I return to China to take over power? Therefore, the prodemocracy movement still has to continue." This is also a pretense remark.

Another said: "We must learn from Sun Yat-sen, the founding father of China, and carry out a violent revolution. But I haven't had time to smuggle guns and ammunition into China. The battle is over so soon?"

Some people even said: "We must learn from India's Mahatma Gandhi and hold a nonviolent and noncooperative movement. But I haven't had time to launch a demonstration in the streets. The battle is over so soon?"

The battle is over. It's really over! All pretense theories should be thrown away. This is a global village, in an internet age! A new international environment and a new level of science and technology are spurring us. There is no need to stick to the rules and waste time. Now that we have a way to win, let's win as soon as possible. Let everyone restore their nature as soon as possible and live an ordinary life as the original common people.

The battle is over! It's really over. At present, only one great person is lacking. He must be chosen by heaven and moved to Washington, DC, to settle down, and it will be done.

The battle is over! It's really over!

December 15, 2019
Washington, DC

6

Guangdong Must Be Independent!

When I returned to New York this time to spend my Christmas holiday, the biggest surprise was that I had finalized the path of Guangdong's independent founding.

I held a secret meeting with the Cantonese and roughly decided on the national flag, the national emblem, the national title, and the national anthem of Guangdong. Then the Guangdong Independence Party will be registered, and there are plans for propaganda, launching, organization, activities, and more.

Guangdong must be independent because in the past two thousand years, Guangdong culture is completely different from that of the Central Plains. Food culture is different; language culture is also different. Many Yankees do not understand Cantonese, and many Cantonese do not understand Mandarin.

Guangdong must be independent because in the past two thousand years, the history of Guangdong is completely different from that of the Central Plains. A group of brutal Yankees, like brutal monkeys, have fought and killed each other every day in order to compete for the throne of a monkey king. Wars and massacres have been endless in the Central Plains. A large number of Central Plains refugees have fled to Guangdong. But in the two thousand years of Guangdong's history, there has been almost no war or famine. In every corner of Guangdong, everyone has been busy earning money for their livelihood. It is normal and not abnormal.

Guangdong must be independent! In the past two thousand years, the wars and famines in Central Plains have led even to cannibalism. However, with no famine in Guangdong history, no cannibalism has occurred in our lovely home. Why should we, civilized Cantonese, accept the rule of you barbaric and cursed northerners?

Guangdong must be independent! The spirit of Cantonese is free. Cantonese people have nothing to do with the world and just want to earn money to support their families. And you cursed people of the north fight for power every day. You are so savage, fighting and killing every day, that sooner or later you will collectively die together. Why must we Cantonese be buried with you?

Guangdong must be independent! This is a matter of international morality. Neighboring countries such as Hong Kong, Taiwan, and Vietnam will be happy to see Guangdong's independence!

Guangdong must be independent. In this way, the issue of the South China Sea will be resolved by the Cantonese. The United States, Japan, Malaysia, Indonesia, the Philippines and other countries, if they hear this good news, will hold a party all night with drinking and dancing and singing!

Guangdong must be independent! I don't know if I might see Guangdong independence in my lifetime, but as long as you want to build a democratic China, we Guangdong people should take the opportunity to become independent. Let's talk about it, you Yankee guys; you have deceived us Cantonese for two thousand years. Over the past two thousand years, you have taken advantage of the Cantonese. In the background of a great unification, we Cantonese are unhappy.

Guangdong must be independent! Two thousand years after the Jews were dispersed, they have still regained their country. Then, we Cantonese can also establish our own country!

Guangdong must be independent! One of the six statutory languages of the United Nations is Cantonese. One of the three major language groups in the United States is Chinese, mostly Cantonese. All overseas Chinese living in Southeast Asian countries speak Cantonese. These Southeast Asian countries do not use English at all and only use their native languages, but Cantonese is unimpeded. Why should we Cantonese devalue ourselves?

Guangdong must be independent! The CCP has already extinguished the Manchurian culture, and it is exterminating the Uyghur culture, Tibetan culture, Hui culture, Hong Kong culture, and Guangdong culture. Why do we Cantonese have to endure the fate of extinction?

7

I Long to Hear about Navarro's Death!

I hear that US President Trump will fly to Beijing this month to pay homage to Chinese emperor Xi Jinping and sign the trade agreement. This marks the end of the US-China trade war. The result is that the United States is defeated and China is victorious.

It's as if a eunuch of the imperial palace wants to feast his friends and relatives, and praises the might of his emperor for cutting off his dick. Being a eunuch is really a matter of glorious ancestors! President Trump is certainly very happy. As if a slave worship his lord with his compliance, President Trump decides to celebrate the US-China trade war with a big event, setting off fireworks, opening champagne, eating and drinking, singing and dancing, and celebrating the America be defeated.

So what will Navarro do? Where will he go? —— This great genius who designed the US-China trade war originally planned to use the trade war to eradicate the Communist forces on this planet. Now, President Trump has decided to completely preserve the evil forces on this planet in order to form a global dictators' club. In 2029, three dictators will emerge on the planet: Trump, Xi Jinping, and Putin. These three dictators will lead the evil forces around the world, and together they will lead all mankind to the dark abyss to suffering for a new millennium.

So what is Navarro to do? Where can he go? —— I think that just resigning is not enough. Four White House minions: Vice President Mike Pence and Secretary of State Michael Richard Pompeo are fart catchers, and John Robert Bolton is a hero who has bandit uphill and has been expelled from the White House, so that now it is Peter Navarro's turn. What will he do, this coward, this silent lamb? Where will he go?

I long to hear about Navarro's death. I long to hear of him dying for his ideals. I long to hear about him committing suicide with a gun! Use this action to stop this unprecedented catastrophe in human history.

I will ask him: "There are over seven billion humans on this planet, and how much effort God has put in to make a great genius like you. Only one philosopher on this planet could conceive of eradicating the evil forces on earth through the trade war. However, the damage that President Trump has caused to the United States is irreversible. If you live a few more years, you can see him establish a news censorship bureau and dissolve Congress and serve a third term as president of the United States. When has he respected you? Does he know that you are one of the ten greatest thinkers of this century? You love being treated like a pet by an emperor; don't you feel ashamed?

I will ask him: "The entire White House has been transformed into a royal palace by President Trump. All senior Washington officials have become ministers of the court. And are you a sex doll in the dormitory? Or are you a funny dwarf before the throne? Why don't you dress yourself up as a laughing clown in the fancy clothes for courtiers to play with? Why do you dress as a timid and melancholy poet in the palace? This kind of insult to the intellectuals is unprecedented, and it is comparable to Qin Shihuang, an ancient Chinese emperor who burned books and buried Confucians.

I will ask him: "President Trump's moral bottom line is this: everything that is conducive to the restoration of monarchy will be done. The trade war you have designed represents the lofty ideal of all humanity to eradicate tyranny on the earth. President Trump is an evil spirit. He will not seek justice for all mankind. 'I am the country. I am the law.' President Trump has always been above the law. In this way, what will the United States look like in the future? The best freedom that the people once enjoyed has gradually disappeared in your times. But you stayed in the White House and assisted a villain in becoming a king. You did not use any moral power to warn him and put up not the slightest resistance to him. You are a devil too. Like this, do you deserve the American people who you have loved?"

I will ask him: "The future of all mankind will gradually become a dark time. As the greatest thinker of our times, you were once a glorious beacon in the history of thought, shining on the thousand-year course of all humankind. However, you let President Trump demolish your lighthouse. You live in the White House like an ant and like a ghost. How should the humans in the next generation worship you?"

So how will I ask him? —— My approach is to give him my books. I am an English writer. I sent my English books, *A*

Chinese Refugee and His American Lovers and *Assassination Tutorial*, into the White House. Because it is a personal gift, the White House Secret Service will transfer it to him after completing the security check. Then I will post the English letter I wrote to him on the internet. Anyone searching for Navarro on the internet will see my question to him.

As soon as President Trump and Emperor Xi Jinping reach a trade agreement, I will ask Navarro: "The rest of your life is about to fade. What will you do in despair?"

However, inciting others to commit suicide is still a criminal offence. But what about this? I have already explained to my good friends Mr. Zhao Yan and Ms. Cai Xiuling: "You must help me. You must testify in the court. You must ask the judge to sentence me to a few more years. I need ten years to be in prison, and then I can complete my PhD in Spanish literature and PhD in mathematics."

What is the most important thing in our life? Knowledge is of course the most important thing. What of life, love, family, money, status, freedom, and health? They are not important. I just want to have a PhD.

I have been living through the ups and downs of suffering, and now working as a blue color in the United States. When can I go to the university to study quietly?

Do you understand? —— You are calling me the national founding father, and I am analyzing to you the methods and steps of overthrowing the CCP. No one on earth can do what I can do. Your inability to overthrow the CCP does not mean that I do not have this ability.

Two years ago, I was going to the White House to launch the inflatable dolls, which were stopped by the prodemocracy predecessors, because the FBI might sue me for offensive crimes. This time, I'm giving my books to Navarro, and the FBI may still sue me for instigating suicide.

It is nothing more than two great thinkers who want to exchange their ideas, articles, and books. If this incident causes one to commit suicide and the other to land in jail, then the United States is fully in control of free speech. The glory of the Statue of Liberty will be extinguished in the United States, and the United States will circulate a new historical farce, just as the ancient Roman Republic gradually became the ancient Roman Empire. The history of all humankind will gradually be brought into a new round of millennium darkness.

January 6, 2020
Washington, DC

8

Trump Can Be Predicted!

Contemporary political scholars believe that US President Trump is unpredictable, acting madly and playing cards completely unreasonably; that is just because they are stupid. As long as they are willing to admit that I am a scientific giant and follow in my footsteps, they will understand that President Trump is completely predictable.

In the past few years, President Trump has been a white mouse in my science laboratory, after I have studied him for several years, and I have completely explored his political laws and thinking mode. I can predict his reaction every step of the way.

Just like Mr. Mendel, the founding father of genetics, who revealed the dominant principle, the separation law, and the free combination law of genetics by planting peas, and also just like geneticist Mr. Morgan who had conducted mutation-induced experiments through the drosophila and obtained the laws of the linkage and the interchange, in the past few years, I have also obtained great achievements in the history of science through observation and research of President Trump.

Scholars in later generations will write eloquent works to

explain Trump Psychology. And I am the originator of Trump Psychology. President Trump is completely predictable under my observation and research. He is also a human. All human beings have their latent modes of thinking and apparent laws of words and deeds. President Trump has not deviated from my scientific discoveries at all! He can be predicted at every step of his actions and planning for governance.

Peas, drosophila, and President Trump are all ordinary experimental objects in the process of scientific practice. They are one of the universal things in the world, and they all have their internal laws and relationships. They can be observed and researched in accordance with scientific methods, and then we can fully grasp their internal dynamics and external behaviors.

With my Trump Psychology, I have become the greatest political thinker in the world, and my achievements have begun to surpass Mr. Navarro, Mr. Graham, Ms. Sheng Xue, and Mr. Zhang Lin.

So how have I explored, enriched, and perfected Trump Psychology in the past few years? As a great scientist, I have four aspects of research achievements in this field. Let me summarize today.

First, I have been the first one to detect the bizarre performance of President Trump and sum it up as the Trump phenomenon. The Trump phenomenon refers to a political phenomenon: the victorious country with absolute superiority must kneel down to greet the defeated country with absolute disadvantage, and bow and kowtow to express his willingness to surrender.

The victorious country must surrender to the defeated

country, that this reality does not exist in human history. In ancient China, a king who won a battle would castrate all the prisoners of war and turn them into his own eunuchs. But President Trump is completely different. After winning the battle, he would castrate himself to become a eunuch, to serve the prisoner of war he defeated, and embrace the prisoner of war as his king. And then, President Trump kneels down to the prisoner of war to worship him as his Lord.

How to explain this completely crazy reality? I have made reasonable explanations in my past works and articles, and summed up this abnormal occurrence as the Trump phenomenon.

Second, I was the first to detect President Trump's mental illness. In my past books and articles, I have introduced President Trump's mental illness in detail. He suffers from mild manic depression, schizophrenia, and dementia.

Third, I was the first to detect President Trump's political behavior pattern, summed him up as the political she-male, and founded the theory of the political she-male.

Samson in the Bible, Dongfang Bubai in *The Swordsman*, and Xiang Yu, the king of Chu in Chinese history, were all great heroes invincible in the world. However, for the love in their hearts, they all willingly died at the hands of the enemies. Their enemies are their lovers. So will President Trump lead the United States to decline and perish for the love in his heart? How to use scientific methods to analyze and research this trend? I have conducted a comprehensive analysis of this proposition in my past works and articles.

Fourth, I was the first to detect President Trump's thinking about his governance and revealed that his dream is restoring the monarchy, predicted his road map and timetable for restoring the monarchy, and commented on the probability of success or failure of his restoration of the monarchy.

President Trump's thoughts on governing the country I have not revealed in detail, so today I will open a new chapter specifically to describe his thoughts on governing the country.

This is indeed an important chapter. How is he going to govern the United States to make things so crazy?

And these seemingly crazy behaviors are completely unpredictable in the eyes of laymen. But I am an insider. As long as I have a clear understanding of his thinking on governing the country, then I can fully predict his various forms of expression in his presidential career for many years to come.

This is a very exciting chapter. Don't miss it!

President Trump's thinking of governing the country coincides with Confucianism, Taoism, and Legalism. It is the same as the political theories of the pre-Qin scholars. The political theories of the ancient Chinese philosophers and sages liked the sea, wide and deep, so much that I can't describe!

Although President Trump has never been edified and nurtured by orthodox Chinese culture in his life, he follows the simplest truths: a sage governing a country should be the internal sage and the external king, rule by inaction, and control the people with the five skills, as in The Book of Lord Shang, etc. These great truths seem to be completely contradictory. However, taking its essence and removing its dross can completely unify a contradictory complex into a perfect individual.

On the surface, the Legalism concept of governing the country and the Confucian concept of governing the country are not the same; like ice and fire, they cannot fit into the same vessel. But in the end Legalism and Confucianism are perfectly combined, forming a ruling mode for more than two thousand years.

These great truths have brought President Trump's political thoughts to the realm of the most brilliant political ideal two thousand years ago.

However, would it be appropriate for an American president to use the Chinese philosophy of two thousand years ago to manage America in the modern high-tech era? —— Of course it is inappropriate. Therefore, President Trump's behavior is seen as crazy and has been criticized. But he is inseparable from it. He is a great patriot! He loves America and the American people deeply. This kind of affection is sincere and true, so he is loved by all American people with so much love and support!

However, what is wrong with using the political level of the Spring and Autumn Period and Warring States Period to govern the contemporary United States? —— The political thinkers in the Spring and Autumn Period and Warring States Period, that is the hundred schools of thought we often talk about, their political ideas are too primitive and crude, and obliterating humanity, and not suitable for contemporary America.

Legalists, Taoists, Mohists, Confucianists, Yin-Yangists, Masters, miscellaneous experts, peasants, novelists, political strategists, military strategists, and physicians in the Spring and Autumn Period and Warring States Period were the most brilliant ideological achievements in the world at that time. Guan Zi, Lao Zi, Confucius, Yan Zi, Sun Zi, Fan Li, Bian Que,

Yin Wen, Lie Zi, Zhuang Zi, Tian Pian, Huang Lao, Yang Zi, Deng Xi, Gong Sun Long Zi, Hui Zi, Gui Gu Zi, Zhang Yi, Su Qin, Sun Bin, Pang Juan, Mencius, Mozi, Gaozi, Shang Yang, Shen Buhu, Shenzi, Xu Xing, Zou Yan, Xunzi, Han Feizi, and Lu Buwei were the most brilliant political thinkers in the world at that time. Isn't it suitable to govern contemporary America with so many theories and ideals of sages in the ancient world? —— Not suitable!

This is because the philosophers of the pre-Qin Dynasty did not have a constitutional concept; nor did they have modern social concepts such as equality, fraternity, human rights, democracy, freedom, justice, science, truth, etc. It is really not suitable to govern contemporary America with the lofty ideal of ruling the country by the sages from two thousand years ago.

When we look back at President Trump's political behavior in recent years, we can summarize his political thinking into five major political ideas: the sage is supreme, the emperor is supreme, the white is supreme, the patriot is supreme, and the people are supreme. These five political ideas are completely consistent with the political theories of the pre-Qin scholars.

A pure and flawless god is most likely the incarnation of an evil devil. This is philosophy.

First, the sage is supreme. According to the doctrines of the pre-Qin philosophers, society basically falls into the categories of scholars, farmers, workers and merchants. The scholar is priority. Then, the sages can only be produced among the scholars, and the sages should govern the United States. And the group of politicians in the US who are members of the Democratic Party are disgraceful and disruptive to the image.

They are not suitable for becoming saints. Therefore, President Trump hates the opposition in the US Congress.

And the American news media, the group of talkative reporters, are not sages. Therefore, President Trump hates journalists.

So who is the greatest sage of our times? The arrogant President Trump certainly considers himself a contemporary sage. The United States must be governed by him, otherwise it will be over! So he just stubbornly uses it for himself, like a patient who avoids doctors and goes madly on his own.

The rule of sages means that President Trump is the contemporary sage, the person chosen by God himself, and he is the chosen one. For him, the heaven will come to the earth.

Therefore, the sages can usurp the throne. If my destiny is mine, I am the king of the earth. President Trump can of course be promoted from a sage to an emperor and establish a lifelong system.

Therefore, if President Trump feels that other presidential candidates do not love the United States as much as he does, they are not suitable to be presidents of the United States. President Trump is free to destroy any presidential candidate by any means. He used this attitude toward former Vice President Biden, who is now the presidential candidate.

Second, the emperor is supreme. According to the doctrine of the Hundred Schools of the pre-Qin Dynasty, I am the emperor, and the purpose of the existence of sages is to maintain the dignity of the emperor. A country with sages should have an emperor. As a result, President Trump's political thinking has continued to move forward and continue on the path of restoring the monarchy. So what is the probability that he will eventually establish the life tenure in the United States? It seems to be only 40 percent. He has a 40 percent chance to serve more than ten years and then die in the White House—just like any emperor in Chinese history who died of old age in the royal palace and must not retire.

Third, the white is supreme. According to the doctrines of the pre-Qin philosophers, an excellence in learning suits an official. Officials are nobles. And those black people in the United States cannot create brilliant achievements in science and art at all, so they are not aristocrats. The aristocracy in the United States can only be composed of the white and Christian. Therefore, the white and Christian governance of the United States is the best governance model.

President Trump is indeed a racist. But there is really nothing wrong with this. In the past two thousand years of human history, the white and Christian led the yellow, the black, Muslim, and Buddhist.

The history of all mankind really proves the truth: The white and Christians are the best! They are indeed better than other races!

Therefore, he naturally has the motivation to exclude Muslims and foreign refugees.

The white is supreme, and thus the nobility is supreme, and the rich are supreme too. Look at President Trump's tax policy. He always cuts the welfare of the poor without increasing taxes on the rich. He likes to rob the poor and help the rich. He believes that the lower class is the low-end population and should be fooled.

The construction of the US-Mexico border wall best reflects President Trump's thinking on governing the country:

sustain white supremacy and retain a small country with few people. This is the essence of his national governance.

A small country with few people is a Taoist political philosophy in ancient China; that is, the emperors of the world should only care about their own country's affairs, not international affairs. It's a pity that life is priceless; still, more and more South American smugglers will go to the sea because of the Trump wall.

After the completion of the Trump wall, the annual smuggling frenzy in the Gulf of Mexico will kill three thousand people, because the human will to pursue freedom is unstoppable.

Fourth, the patriot is supreme. According to the doctrine of the pre-Qin philosophers, I am the country, for I am the king. Under the sky, the world is mine, and the subjects are mine too. A complete country should have an emperor. Then the emperor should be patriotic because the country is the emperor's personal property.

Only a country with an emperor can be a complete country, just as a family with a father is a complete family. The people are like orphans, and the emperor is like a father. Fathers will love their children, and the emperors will love their subjects. Therefore, as a great patriot, President Trump will inevitably love the United States and the American people until his death. He wants to do everything possible to protect and nurture the United States and the American people. So let the American people have an emperor.

Is it any wonder that President Trump continues to impose tariffs on China, Europe, Japan, Canada, and other countries and organizations? He considers himself the emperor, and the emperor should protect the royal property. American tariffs are the emperor's royal property. How can the emperor's property be distributed to the folk?

The clearest manifestation of President Trump's patriotic complex is also his most bizarre political behavior: quarreling with the internal and surrendering to the external.

Quarreling with the internal is in line with the Confucian doctrine that only the women and the villains are difficult to raise. The representatives in the US Congress are all the women and the villains, and they are unbearable. President Trump himself is the most devout Christian, a humble gentleman who is upright by God, who is honest and fearless. So how can he not torment them?

Surrendering to the external is also in line with the Taoist doctrine of a small country with few people. The United States and other countries in the world are equal and mutually beneficial countries. The emperors of various countries should manage their countries well. Therefore, the United States cannot bully any rogue country with the reputation of human rights. Even if China steals American technology, as long as it doesn't kill American soldiers, that is no big deal, and all is trivial. So he saved ZTE and Huawei, allowing China to continue to infiltrate and corrupt the United States.

Fifth, the people are supreme. According to the doctrines of the pre-Qin philosophers, an emperor should love the people like his children. An emperor should love his subjects under his rule, cherish the people, and be sympathetic to the people. This is absolutely no problem! President Trump, as a good emperor, embodies the emperor's kindness and compassion. In particular, his series of domestic tax policies, health care policies, refugee policies, etc., all reflect his love for American citizens.

His love for the people is hierarchical. In Confucianism, Confucius also expressed clearly that there is a difference in love.

In Confucianism, the master and the slave are relative, forming the ruling class and the ruled class. In the eyes of President Trump, American citizens are the masters of the United States. Green card holders, refugees, and foreign tourists who appear in the United States all have begun to be called lesser people, or gangsters, and or slaves. The lords and the slaves should not have equal rights.

In the political philosophy of the Democratic Party of the United States, the rights of citizenship are granted only to American citizens, while other benefits such as education, medical care, employment, relief, etc., can be granted to any resident living in the United States. But President Trump followed Confucianism and believed that American citizens are the masters and American refugees are hooligans and cannot be treated equally. He has wanted to build a wall between the masters and the servants to clear the boundaries so as not to produce the evil slaves to hurt the masters.

But the general understanding in philosophy is that the master and the slave are relative, interchangeable, and cannot be rigidly confirmed. You are the master in this category, and you may also be the slave in another category. In dealing with the phenomenon of the evil slaves hurting the masters, and the phenomenon of the evil masters hurting the slaves, the best solution is through religion and belief. In other words, under the principles and standards of Christ's great love, everyone should forgive and tolerate each other.

It is not the best way to use political means to forcibly end the phenomenon of the evil slaves hurting the masters and the evil masters hurting the slaves.

Foreign refugees take advantage of American citizens, the blacks take advantage of the whites, Muslims take advantage of Christians, lazy people take advantage of hardworking people, and fools take advantage of smart people. —— This, in the United States, is indeed an ironclad fact. Therefore, President Trump believes that this is a phenomenon of the evil slaves hurting the masters, and political means must be used to resolve it. This is not wrong, but it is not the best solution.

Next, let me lead you to make predictions about President Trump's political behavior in the next few years.

After I have detected President Trump's thinking on governance, I can completely predict his political trends and behavior in the next few years. After I discovered his statecraft, it was easy. As long as you throw away the excessive modern thinking accumulated in your mind and go back to the ancient times and observe President Trump with the thoughts of the pre-Qin philosophers, you can completely predict him.

All his political behaviors are completely consistent with the political ideals of the pre-Qin philosophers two thousand years ago!

So sometimes, I like to say that he is a lunatic. He is really a lunatic. How can an American living in the contemporary era govern the United States with ancient Chinese political ideas two thousand years ago? —— But from another perspective, who can say that he is really a lunatic? He is completely normal! He did business with the management methods of the pre-Qin scholars of two thousand years ago. His business is very successful, and he is a billionaire. Therefore, the political thoughts of the pre-Qin schools of thought are invincible truths!

It is indeed true that every businessman's behavior pattern is completely in line with the doctrines of the pre-Qin scholars. Who can say that the doctrines of the pre-Qin schools of thought are outdated?

Let's try to analyze Trump's diplomatic behavior using the political thoughts of the pre-Qin scholars.

Chinese emperor Xi Jinping is a bosom friend of President Trump. What does a bosom friend do? They should help each other. Therefore, President Trump will help Xi Jinping consolidate his throne and support Xi Jinping's iron-fisted suppression of Hong Kong, Xinjiang, Tibet, Falun Gong, Christianity, etc.

As long as Xi Jinping does not cross the border to kill American soldiers, President Trump will support him to the end.

North Korean Emperor Kim Jong-un is also a bosom friend of President Trump. What does a bosom friend do? They should help each other. Therefore, President Trump will help Kim Jong-un consolidate his throne. As long as Kim Jong-un does not cross the border to kill American soldiers, President Trump will support him to the end.

However, the Iranian emperor Ali Khamenei is really not friendly enough. He actually asked those Iranian generals to kill American soldiers. This seriously violates the principle of loving the slaves like his own children in Confucianism, and President Trump wants to be a good emperor and will never allow any foreign emperor to kill American soldiers. Therefore, President Trump did not hesitate to turn his face against Khamenei!

Taoism's doctrine, the Tao De Jing, mentioned the best state of governance: we can hear the sounds of our chickens and dogs in the neighborhood, but don't communicate with each other until old and dying. —— This is the best situation of state relations, that is, a small country with few people. Today, we live in a common global village, and the developments of science and technology have made the world's space very narrow. The earth should indeed be restored to a small country with few people. The emperors of each country manage their own country well, and that is enough. We can rest assured to establish a global dictators' club on the earth, so that emperors from all over the world can enjoy their lives.

Originally, President Trump only wanted to rule by doing nothing to be a good emperor in peace and to manage the United States. Unexpectedly, the Iranian emperor wanted to kill American soldiers, which caused President Trump to get angry. He did not hesitate to suppress Ali Khamenei, threatening him, claiming to deprive him of his emperor qualification and expel him from the global dictators' club.

President Trump's ambitions are to restore the monarchy in the United States and to establish a global dictators' club. The prospect of this wish is very bright and optimistic. By 2030, the earth will still be ruled by emperors such as Trump, Putin, Xi Jinping, Kim Jong-un, Bashar, Maduro, Khamenei, etc., and the world will be peaceful, colorful, and wonderful; isn't that the best?

But the impeachment of the US House of Representatives has reduced President Trump's ambitions a lot. The Speaker of the House, Mrs. Nancy Pelosi, performed well enough to be called a national heroine in American history. She bravely stopped the crazy actions of President Trump. This has greatly reduced the probability of President Trump's success in restoring the monarchy, so that the current probability of success is only 40 percent.

However, the people are always foolish and misled. President Trump is like Emperor Caesar of the ancient Roman Republic. The American people will gradually realize that if they cannot support President Trump forever to make him an emperor, the United States will lose its momentum and direction. After all, President Trump will succeed on the royal throne.

By 2030, more and more emperors will appear on the earth. Every emperor loves his country's people, and all dictators are united and working together to build a global village. Then the earth will become better and better under the leadership of President Trump and other emperors.

Every emperor is a red sun. On the earth, there are more and more red suns, which will never set. The night is gone, the earth is always beautiful and bright. What a wonderful world the future is!

Therefore, if we liberals want to rebel against the monarchy and play the game of shooting the sun as in ancient Chinese mythology, we actually commit a disrespectful crime!

Remember, predicting Trump is a professional expertise. This knowledge has been founded by me. I founded the Trump Psychology.

Here, I would like to invite you to review the commentary of an ancient poem, "Some Cucumbers on a Yellow Balcony," by Mr. Li Ka-shing, the richest Chinese businessman. Mr. Li Ka-shing said: "The best cause will bear the worst result." What does this philosophical saying indicate? It indicates that US President Trump, who loves the United States infinitely, is actually one of the most dangerous traitors ever to betray the United States!

President Trump is a great patriot! His patriotism and love for the people are sincere and true, just like that of a pure child! —— But he is from hell! In the twenty-first century, a contemporary American president is carrying the soul of a philosopher who lived two thousand years ago, likes an evil ghost who has just crawled out of the grave!

As long as you all study Trump Psychology well, restore the entire state of mind to the political ideals of the philosophers of two thousand years ago, and completely throw away modern political ideas, you can completely predict all of President Trump's political actions in the years to come!

Go ahead. Go and restore your wisdom to an idiot state. And think of a way about the national affairs like the sages two thousand years ago. Being an ancient sage, in this way, you can completely connect with President Trump and will be in harmony with each other!

Everything that President Trump has done is consistent with the political wisdom of two thousand years ago; that is a philosophical achievement worthy of the ancient Chinese sages.

Please use the political and historical concepts of the ancient slave society to understand President Trump. Don't use the democratic and human rights concepts of modern society.

Then you will understand his words, deeds, behaviors, and thoughts at a glance.

When you regard him as a slave owner or king of two thousand years ago, you will praise him and admire him for how his warm, patriotic love for the people makes him diligent and hardworking for the people, of the people, by the people. He is so compassionate toward the people, devoted to the people, and well-intentioned for the people.

He is our merciful emperor! He is our holy lord and our sacred king in our prosperous epoch!

January 8, 2020
Washington, DC

9

I Am the Founder of Trump Psychology

I want to summarize and review with you, and check my transcript by the way.

I fled overseas in 2015. Now, in 2020, after five years, I still maintain the level and the ability of a great scholar. I established three academic systems: Escape Studies, Assassination Studies, and Trump Psychology.

I am the founder of Escape Studies, and I am known as an Escape Master. At present, this academic system covers all the dead ends of the escaping career. As long as a Chinese wants to escape from China, there must be a way.

In my opinion, the livelihood of the Chinese people is for preparing to escape from where he lives to his death.

I think that dying in a foreign country is happier than living in China.

For the Chinese, death is a kind of happiness. Therefore, I encourage the Chinese people to die on the way to escape.

I am the founder of Assassination Studies. I wrote a book entitled *Assassination Tutorial*. I am the godfather of assassination.

But the assassination knowledge I talked about in the book belongs to the category of social assassination.

Recently, the US army assassinated Iran's General Soleimani, which belongs in the category of military assassinations.

In the future, the Army's West Point Military Academy, the Air Force Academy, and the Naval Academy of the United States will teach courses on military assassinations. I hope my *Assassination Tutorial* can be placed in the libraries of those military colleges. I hope those generals and soldiers still respect me as the godfather of assassination.

Because I am the pioneer of assassination theory.

I am the founder of Trump Psychology. Trump Psychology belongs to both a theoretical branch of political science and to psychology.

Politics and psychology meet perfectly in Trump Psychology.

With Trump Psychology, all the weird and abnormal behaviors of President Trump can completely predict his future performance and answer his current motives. His words, deeds, and thoughts have no blind spots and are completely covered, explaining him completely.

Trump Psychology has four theoretical pillars.

First, the Trump phenomenon.

Trump Phenomenon refers to the fact that a victorious country with absolute advantage must kneel down to kowtow in surrender and to ask for mercy from a defeated country which is at an absolute disadvantage.

This phenomenon has never existed in the past, is unprecedented, and is the original creation of President Trump.

Second, President Trump's mental illness. He suffers from mild manic depression, schizophrenia, and dementia.

Third, the theory of the political she-male.

The theory of the political she-male is inspired by a martial arts novel, *The Swordsman*, written by Mr. Jin Yong of Hong Kong. In his book, an invincible greatest hero Dongfang Bubai is undefeated; however, he has wielded a sword to castrate himself for studying mysterious martial arts. And the end, he decides to die for his admired enemy, Ms. Ren Yingying, a beautiful girl.

President Trump is a political ladyboy. Spiritually, he has wielded a sword to castrate himself for worshipping the enemies. In the end, the powerful military resources of the United States are just a pile of scrap iron, and President Trump will lead the United States on a path of decline and destruction.

Fourth, I detected President Trump's thinking on governance. His political ambitions are twofold. First, establishing a global dictators' club. Second, restoring the monarchy in the United States.

In order to realize his political ambitions, he will do whatever it takes to commit crimes at all costs.

Looking back at my transcript, I feel that in the past five years, my academic achievements are still tremendous—even though I am alone, but I will be forever.

Can I look down on future generations and generations of humans?

What do you think?

January 19, 2020
Washington, DC

Here are some books I have published.

10

The Reasons for Mrs. Nancy Pelosi's Failure

As a great prophet, before the impeachment case entered the proceedings, I had predicted many times that the Speaker of the House of Representatives, Mrs. Nancy Pelosi would be defeated by US President Trump. Everyone has been witnessing my prophecy. Over the past few months, I have been conducting multiple analyses on this impeachment case. Now, the impeachment case is as I predicted: Mrs. Nancy Pelosi has been defeated. So let's summarize the reasons for the failure of Mrs. Nancy Pelosi in order to improve our political analysis skills.

There are five major factors that could make Mrs. Nancy Pelosi lose in the impeachment case. These five factors, as long as any one of them takes effect, Mrs. Nancy Pelosi could win the impeachment case. Unfortunately, it is destined that the United States should collapse. None of the factors is effective.

These five factors are as follows.

First, she has no tenacious fighting spirit.

This is completely conceivable. Mrs. Nancy Pelosi was born in a scholarly family and is an elegant lady. Mr. Trump was born behind a boxing club, and he is a villain. So how can they attack each other? She has already lost a lot of strength, toughness, viciousness, and sinister confidence. It doesn't matter that she doesn't need to fight. If she does fight, she must lose.

Second, she has no strategy or tactics.

Originally, the House of Representatives had passed the impeachment case of President Trump, that as long as she stayed calm and waited patiently, she can brew a perfect plan of action. But she submitted it to the Senate too early. She should wait another six months and submit it to the Senate this summer. At that time, it was the crucial moment for canvassing votes! At that time, she can pierce his throat with a sword and kill President Trump at once! Unfortunately, she is not fierce enough.

President Trump has lied and done all manner of bad things. He tells lies every day. He does bad things every month. Regarding the impeachment case as a sword hanging over his head, and delaying cutting him down, let him show his ugliness first, and then suddenly attack him at a critical moment, and he can be strangled. Unfortunately, she is not decisive enough.

Third, she has no ideological weapons.

How to Extinguish Americans? This book was written by me. It is a very powerful thought weapon. I only need to give this thought weapon to Mrs. Nancy Pelosi, and she will take this book to the US Congress to promote it, and it will kill President Trump.

How to Extinguish Americans? This book introduces President Trump's goals. There are two goals for his struggle. First, restoring the monarchy in the United States. Second, establishing a global dictators' club. Mrs. Nancy Pelosi only needs to tell all members of Congress that President Trump is trying to restore the monarchy. Then all members of Congress will immediately abandon him.

Unfortunately, I cannot publish this book until the end of this year at the earliest. Now I have to work part-time, too late to write and to translate it.

Therefore, the current Mrs. Nancy Pelosi has no ideological weapons, and it is destined to be the United States.

Fourth, she has no conspiracy.

She is a Catholic, and her political methods used are too bright, too fair, and too pure. This is doomed to result in her failure.

Political struggle needs political means. In the process of confronting President Trump, she did not plan to disintegrate the enemy camp and launch the counter-rebellion. She should secretly communicate with some members of the Republican Party of the United States and ask them to stage a collective mutiny, so that President Trump can be strangled.

Fifth, she has no foresight.

She is too naive. She actually looked forward to this year's election. It's just a nerve. Think about it, everyone: since President Trump has disallowed a fair impeachment, how can he allow a fair election?

This year's general election will be unfair. In this year's unfair election, only President Trump can be reelected, and other candidates will inevitably lose.

So how will President Trump succeed in being reelected as president of the United States this November?

First, he will launch a god-making movement. The American people will always understand that President Trump is the beloved son of God and is a sun god in the world. If there were no Trump on the earth, it would be like a polar night. As a result, the suppressed media now have vent channels, and they will rush to publicize: Long live the Red Sun, long live Trump, long live the Trump Dynasty, forever!

Second, he will purge the dissidents. Russian dictator Putin is only alone and has assassinated two hundred political enemies. So is President Trump also preparing to assassinate his political opponents in the United States? Not for now. But he would attack indirectly, intimidate, and persuade through relatives and friends of the political opponents. As a result, all political opponents participating in the election will eventually have an accident and cede the presidency to President Trump.

Third, he will cheat in elections. What will be done if all the conspiracies are exhausted and President Trump still loses the election? That will be easy. In this impeachment, the political brokers took money from the Chinese government and bribed each senator one by one; that was indeed a very heavy workload. However, in this election, things are much simpler. Elections in the United States are controlled by the Elections Commission. Thus, President Trump will greet the chairman of the Elections Commission, who will be frightened by his presidential power and welcome him. So with some tricks, President Trump will surely be reelected this year.

It's over. America is over. Mrs. Nancy Pelosi was defeated in this impeachment case, and since then, the United States will never have a chance to survive. President Trump's destruction of the American political system is irreversible! Since then, the United States has forever moved toward autocracy. The democratic and free America has disappeared forever. It is destined, that the United States should end.

It's over. America is over. She will never be able to come back to life.

After fifty years, the United States will become a very authoritarian country, exporting countless American refugees to the world. But in the next fifty years, how will the United States gradually fall into an authoritarian country? At present, a new political storm is brewing in American politics to overthrow the dictatorship of President Trump. However, the general situation has passed, and the recovery is weak. It is estimated that in the next fifty years, the United States will experience three dictators, forming three political shock waves, and become an authoritarian country. Trump is only the first shock wave.

It is as if the ancient Roman Republic had transformed into the Roman Empire, and the United States is declining step by step. However, in the next fifty years, is there really no great hero who will turn out to save the United States? And how many steps will it take to turn her into an authoritarian country?

I will continue to give you some academic guidance. It is destined that America has been damned.

February 2, 2020
Washington, DC

11

Escaping: Three Cases

In the second half of last year, three of my good friends fled to the United States: Mr. Neo, Mr. Wang Kaiming, and Mr. Wang Ying-gou. I want to introduce their stories in the United States, and let everyone understand and adapt to the new escape situation.

First, Mr. Neo.

He had studied and worked in Germany before he fled to the United States. He is fluent in Chinese, English, and German. Last summer, US President Trump showed a series of abnormal phenomena, which confused the political direction of the United States extremely. Is the democratic system of the United States going forward, standing still, or going backward? I am extremely unclear. So I persuaded him tactfully not to flee to the United States and instead flee to Germany.

But he regarded me as a relative. Because a Chinese who flees overseas often falls into a state of unaccompanied loneliness, they will be attached to their first overseas correspondent. My lofty character and profound knowledge attracted him. He was willing to come close to me and spend the rest of his life with me, and we could take care of, and depend on, and comfort each other forever like relatives.

I kept rejecting him, but I couldn't talk to him about the mutation phenomenon in the United States. Because he was afraid that he would be arrested by the police in mainland China, he rarely dared to go over the firewall and chat with me. He was always hidden.

Then he really had no hesitation and fled to the United States. At that time, the political situation in the United States was becoming clearer. President Trump had decided to turn the United States into an authoritarian country. As a result, my mood became even heavier. I had hurt him. I resolutely rejected him, refused to accept him, and let him flee to Germany in despair.

Today, he has settled down in the United States. My guilt for him is deepened. This is because I know that in fifty years, his grandchildren will not be able to endure the tyranny of the United States, so they will pack up and flee from the United States.

Second, Mr. Wang Kaiming.

He turned out to be a talented man in mainland China, but he fled because of official suppression. Fortunately, he escaped to my side at the right time. At that time, President Trump had already decided to turn the United States into an authoritarian country. The situation is completely clear. However, when I took him to visit all the prodemocracy leaders in Washington, DC, they all persuaded him to stay in the United States.

I am the only exception. I yelled at him: "A tiger won't eat its children. Why should you listen to the nonsense of those idiots? Those idiots want to kill your family. Why do you want to kill yourself? America must become an autocratic country.

If your children are geniuses, then they must be killed. Why do you want your offspring to die?"

After I scolded him, he suddenly woke up. Because he himself is also a genius, he knew how much the CCP wanted to kill him in the past. Then if the United States becomes an authoritarian country, his offspring will also be killed. So he immediately followed my advice and fled to Canada.

Watching him escape to Canada, my heart was very happy. This was my most satisfying rescue operation last year. Since then, his family will live and work in Canada for generations, and there is no need to flee again.

Third, Mr. Wang Ying-gou.

He has been my comrade in arms for many years. We met in Shenzhen, China, and we were also anti-Communists together.

When I fled to the United States in 2015, he was extremely envious of me. Unfortunately, he was charged by the frontier and could not go. Who knows, at the end of last year, he suddenly contacted me and said he had arrived in Los Angeles, America. When I heard it, I felt sad. President Trump is restoring the monarchy, and the United States is destined to become a tyranny. "Why did you escape to the United States?"

Once, in the first half of last year, Mr. Xianglin told me that Mr. Wang Ying-gou had been to Japan and had looked for him. However, Japan is a constitutional monarchy, and the political situation will be stable for the next hundred years without tyranny. His best place to stay should be Japan, staying with Mr. Xianglin. In the future, Japan will always be a happy country. But the United States will suffer political turmoil and social unrest continuously.

Tomorrow, I will fly to Las Vegas to attend the Third Congress of the Federation for a Democratic China (FDC). I also invited Mr. Wang Ying-gou to attend. At that time, when I see him, should I scold him? "My Escape Studies are truth and science. I am an escape master. "Why didn't you respect my knowledge? Why didn't you seek my opinion before you fled? Why did you escape to Japan and then turn to the United States?"

There is a lingo in economics that if you do not obey the laws of the economy, you will be punished by the laws of the economy. Similarly, if you don't comply with Escape Studies, you will also be punished by Escape Studies. How will I punish Mr. Wang Ying-gou? I will punish his grandchildren to run into the raging sea and flee from the United States to escape tyranny.

There is a law in my Escape Studies: no tyrant, no refugees. Today, the United States is producing dictators, and there will be more and more dictators in the future. Then, Americans can only gradually become refugees in the next fifty years and flee to the countries without tyrants.

Neo, Wang Kaiming, Wang Ying-gou. United States, Canada, United States. Guilt, happiness, sadness. The three fugitives brought me three feelings. I just want to advise those who are quasi-fugitives that in the future, the best destinations for escape are Canada, Australia, and New Zealand. Those three countries will not have tyranny in the next hundred years, enough for your children and grandchildren to live in and work there.

Let's take a look at what a great historical figure I am. I am an escaping master. For the past five years, I have been teaching everyone to escape from China. In the fifty years after my death, I will have left writings to teach you how to escape from the United States. I am benefiting the fugitives for generations and generations.

The earth is so small. I will show you where is your home is and which method will ensure your escape. The happiness of thousands upon thousands of human beings, are led by me. I am amazing.

February 6, 2020
Washington, DC

12

Road Map and Timetable of China's Democratic Process

The headquarters of the Democratic Party of China is in New York, and its chairman is Dr. Wang Juntao. Now, some party members have asked me a sharp question: "If you do not tell us about the road map and timetable for overthrowing the CCP, we will no longer call you the founding father of New China."

I like everyone calling me the founding father of the nation because Guangdong's independence will become the biggest barrier against interference in Hong Kong's independence, thus protecting Hong Kong more effectively. I like to protect Hong Kong.

I like being assassinated by the Ministry of State Security of China, because I am so old and have never achieved anything in my whole life. I think to be assassinated would be great, dying at such a glorious peak of life. And the independence career must face assassination. I like it.

Everything is what I like. I like this life of licking blood and cutting off the enemy's heads. If all Chinese in the world liked living their lives that way, China would have realized democracy long ago.

Then I will announce the road map and timetable for over-throwing the CCP.

This Thanksgiving, Mr. Wang Kaiming and I went to a friend's house for dinner. At dinner, Mr. Wang Kaiming also asked the same question: "Tell me, how are you going to return to Guangdong to be the founding father of the nation?"

Everyone's thought is: *How do you build your team, like Sun Yat-sen?*

However, I was confident and told everyone with serious-ness: "Isn't that a very simple thing? I just have to go back to Guangdong and tell them. I'm just a poor man with no money. But each of you is a rich man with at least several billions. I want to tell them that after a four-year term of office, I will return to the United States for retirement, and Guangdong will still be managed by you. I will leave Guangdong forever after only four years to establish a democratic structure. You see. Look, do you want me to be your founding father? If you don't want it, I'll leave you, ignore you, and let you die in a vendetta, and your family will be destroyed."

When I said this, everyone was immediately dumbfounded, bowed their heads, and said nothing. Everyone but Mr. Wang Kaiming, who laughed when he heard it and asked everyone, "Do you understand?"

Because no one knew whether I was joking, they didn't know what to say. Did my words seem to be telling a fairy tale from a dream? Would I just take a plane flight back to Guangdong so I could be the founding father of Guangdong? What are the methods and steps? No one knew. In human history, is there a better joke than this?

Only Mr. Wang Kaiming understood. In my speech, in

fact, the road map and timetable for realizing democracy in China were all set out together!

This road map puts the finishing touches on two political mysteries: First, the democratic movement and the independence movement are intertwined and identical. They are first and last, they are both top and bottom, and they go hand in hand. To engage in democracy is to engage in independence! To engage in democracy is to engage in division too! As long as we want to realize democracy in China, we must disintegrate China and realize the independence of Guangdong.

Second, China's corrupt officials are the backbone of China's democracy movement. The overseas democracy movement teams are just a miscellaneous army and guerrilla force and can only do superficial work on the sidelines; that is not the backbone of China's democratic process. The prodemocracy tycoons in mainland of China are just a group of living dead in the Zhongnan Mountains. They are a motley crew in China's prisons. They can only wait to die in captivity. There is no need to confirm their power in the Chinese democracy movement.

China's corrupt officials are the backbone of China's democracy movement. In other words, the success or the failure of the Chinese democratic movement depends entirely on whether it can mobilize the political levers to promote a coup in Beijing. Only when China's corrupt officials participate in a coup can China achieve democracy.

This view is very similar to Mr. Wei Jingsheng, the godfather of the Chinese democracy movement. I believe that many prodemocracy leaders agree with this point of view. In other words, the overseas prodemocracy movement is actually a propaganda and an academic activity, not a political move-ment. It cannot seize power and cannot shake the foundation of the CCP's rule.

We take to the streets to demonstrate and to protest be-cause of only our conscience. We are just a group of ordinary people. If you think the common people can overthrow the CCP, that would be foolish.

As for the timetable for overthrowing the CCP, I also made it clear. The overseas prodemocracy leaders are unable to over-throw the CCP. They are only doing some prodemocracy ac-tivities out of the need of their conscience, in order to refresh their reason for existence. So if I don't plan to overthrow the CCP in the next ten years, I will ask them to buy the coffins, choose the graves, and bury them in the United States.

The domestic prodemocracy leaders are also unable to overthrow the CCP. They are just a group of the living dead, living in a tomb in the Zhongnan Mountains without the sun, and they will not reappear under the sky. Then, if I don't plan to overthrow the CCP in the next ten years, I will ask them to buy the ash boxes, burn them into ashes, and bury them in China.

So who can overthrow the CCP? —— Simplify the prob-lem completely. Who can cause a coup in Beijing?

Only the president of the United States!

As long as the president of the United States adjusts its China policy slightly, a coup will occur in Beijing.

How to kill Xi Jinping? —— The American thinker Navarro proposed a plan, the US-China trade war. US Senator Rubio proposed another plan to sanction Xi Jinping through the Bill of Rights. Mr. Wang Kaiming put forward three plans, and I also put forward two plans. However, four people and seven plans all failed. President Trump will never kill Xi Jinping!

Here is how this timetable for overthrowing the CCP was calculated. In 2020, if President Trump is reelected, then China will not have democracy in 2024. President Trump will defend the Xi Dynasty until his death and will give Taiwan to Xi Jinping as a tribute to an emperor from a vassal.

So from 2024 to 2029, as long as I am alive, I will call on the president of the United States to facilitate a coup in Beijing, okay?

13

Will President Trump Assassinate Us?

(An Announcement of The Global Gourmet Association)

Dear foodies, hello. We have some gourmet information to tell everyone.

Mr. Wen Yunchao has decided to hold a banquet for some friends in New York in three consecutive days. Anyone can sign up with him. As long as the news is confirmed that President Trump has lost the election at the end of this year, he will invite you to attend the banquet.

Mr. Li Xiangyang has also decided to hold a similar banquet for some friends in San Francisco. Anyone can sign up with him. As long as the news is confirmed that President Trump has lost the election at the end of this year, he will invite you to attend the banquet too.

I have also decided to hold a banquet for some friends in Memphis, which anyone can sign up for. As long as the news is confirmed that President Trump has lost the election at the end of this year, I will invite you to attend the banquet. Please fly to Tennessee for the dinner.

It won't cost much. On the farm where I will be living,

there is a lake and a river. If I go fishing for ten large bass, I can host a barbecue dinner.

There are chickens on the farm, and potatoes are grown. How about I make another big pot of potato chicken soup?

In addition, I ask the hens to lay a few more eggs to make a large plate of French Niçoise salad. Okay?

There are also various vegetables grown on the farm, suitable for a cold dressing, a stir-fry, or a soup, I will prepare meals for ten people.

Grapes are still planted on the farm, and the wine we have made by ourselves can be supplied in unlimited quantities. Then, when we are drunk and full, we can take off our shoes and dance and sing on the wooden pavilion next to the lotus pond, like country cowboys.

At that time, in the hazy evening, the gentle moon on the sky, the warm bonfire under the fir, the curling fireworks above the villa will create a romantic movie scene. This lifestyle is leisurely and fascinating, and it is completely consistent with the ancient farming life. It is a classic picture straight from a Hollywood romance film. I will play khushtar for everyone, and then start playing guitar and singing. Poetry, wine, food, and music will weave a splendid and intoxicating American dream in the blossoming manor.

The most authentic lifestyle for Americans is so simple and primitive, authentic and natural.

We live in the United States as if in a fairy tale world.

Well, we are already preparing for the food festivals in New York, San Francisco, and Memphis. So who will host the food festivals in Los Angeles, Seattle, Chicago, Miami, Washington, DC, New Orleans, Boston and other cities? Please register; all the city owners, let us hold a global food festival together. In this way, let's eat and drink and make the earth a joyful ocean. Our lives are so happy—who can take it off?

I believe Sister Jasmine will be happy to hold this kind of food festival in Sweden. So who will hold the food festivals in else major cities of all around the world, such as London, Berlin, Paris, Rome, Tokyo, Bangkok, Sydney, and Toronto? Please also sign up, all the major city owners, and let's have a carnival together. Okay?

This time the food event is very important. If it cannot be held smoothly, then the United States will move toward autocracy. Autocratic countries always want to restore the monarchy. And along with the monarchy come the slavery system and the assassination system.

It is not easy to maintain an autocratic rule; it is impossible to maintain an autocratic rule without establishing an assassination system. In 1997, I wrote to the Legislative Council members of Hong Kong, Mr. Li Cheuk-ren and Mr. Tu Jinshen, telling them: "Hong Kong's return to the motherland will inevitably flow into a river of blood and rush a pile of corpses!" But the two lawmakers ignored my advice and thought it would never come to that. A thriving Hong Kong, who wants to kill it? Hong Kong people were celebrating their return to the motherland.

However, my prophecy still worked. This time the Hong Kong anti-transmission movement, the Chief Executive Mrs. Carrie Lam Cheng Yuet-ngor, in a rage, assassinated 10,000 Hong Kong people. The total amount of assassinations on such a large scale is due to the CCP sending a special force to Hong Kong, commonly known as a zombie troop. Using the army to carry out the assassination activities will of course cause a lot of casualties.

It is called a zombie troop because its training base is in a mountainous area in Jiangxi Province, China. The long-term isolation, the constant brainwashing, and the terrifying and suffocating life as if a tomb kept the soldiers completely ignorant and turned them into the walking dead. They are just a group of zombies, without any personal will. They are no longer humans, just some killing machines. They only obey the party's words and have completely lost human emotions. In order to maintain the party's rule, these killers can even assassinate their parents, wives, and children.

Zombie troops are handed over to the army establishment. At the beginning of its establishment, its imaginary enemy was the demonstrators. Therefore, its killers did not need to learn to use weapons and shoot. Their daily training is to practice fighting and grappling. What is repeated every day is the practice of how to use a hundred methods to kill people with their bare hands and turn a living person into a dead body in three seconds.

Generally speaking, after five years of unarmed training, the killers are basically fully qualified in thought, physical stamina, and skills. They can all turn a living person into a dead body within three seconds.

So will the United States learn from the CCP and form a zombie troop? It can't do it. The US Department of Defense has a variety of military assassination teams with a wide range of arms; the FBI has a large number of snipers too, and the CIA is more secretive with countless assassinating methods and experts who can use poison and kill many people in invisible ways, They can also make the enemy completely evaporate in silence, instantly making him colorless, tasteless, and odorless, and missing. —— However, these three US government departments are unwilling to stir up this mess to carry out assassination activities in the United States.

Then, to restore the monarchy, the only way is to let the US Department of Justice outsource the assassination mission to an employment company. However, in this way, the scale of the assassinations will be very limited and can only reach the levels seen in Russia and Venezuela. President Putin of Russia assassinated some two hundred political enemies, and President Maduro of Venezuela assassinated three hundred. If President Trump of the United States wants to restore the monarchy, he can only assassinate hundreds of political enemies in the United States.

The first wave of assassinations will be the members of US Congress and journalists. Monarchy is always promoted with slavery. The members of the US Congress are unwilling to become ministers of an emperor, and American journalists are also unwilling to become an emperor's slaves. If they are disobedient, they should be killed. The second wave of assassination blacklists points to those of us gourmets who organize these food events.

Therefore, if we cannot hold a food festival this year, then Mr. Wen Yunchao, Mr. Li Xiangyang, and I will have to flee from the United States in 2025; otherwise we will be killed.

There is an interesting phenomenon that I want to tell everyone. Is China an authoritarian country without an assassination system? No, China has a conventional assassination system, which is called a live organ harvesting system. That is also an assassination system. In addition, China has an unjust prison system and the concentration camps system as additional means of massacre. China's foodies can be served by the unjust prison system. Chinese gourmets are safer than American gourmets and will not be assassinated.

I was originally your assassination godfather and wrote a book, *Assassination Tutorial.* Of course I have to clarify the knowledge of assassination for you.

So what kind of organization is A Global Resistance against Restoration of Monarchy Alliance? This is a virtual organization on the internet. President Trump has two political goals: the first is to restore the monarchy in the United States, and the second is to establish an emperor's club in the worldwide. Since our organization is going to fight against the restoration of the monarchy, this year, it can only take food activities to counter his assassination activities.

Our food festival this year is to wish President Trump to be arrested and imprisoned. The general political law is like this: as long as President Trump loses the election this year, within three years, the new US president will inevitably order to arrest him. Therefore, President Trump must win this year's election. This is also an act of self-defense. Who wants to go to jail?

I wish you all have happy hours and a good time together. Then designate the day when President Trump loses the election as Bacchus Day, and make everyone celebrate. We must follow the great ideal of Epicureanism and enjoy our cheerful life!

A representative from Washington, DC, of A Global Resistance against Restoration of Monarchy Alliance

March 2, 2020
Washington, DC

14

To Mr. Navarro

Dear Mr. Navarro, hello.

I am a writer from China, now settled in Washington, DC, the capital of the United States. As a tribute to you, I am mailing you my three books as a gift.

In my prose collection, *Rainbow Will Rise Up*, my dedication reads: "You have watched Uighurs being slaughtered like a movie, and watched Hong Kongers being slaughtered like a movie too. Nowadays, you are watching Americans being slaughtered like a movie. Are you satisfied? Are you a coward?"

In my novel, *A Chinese Refugee and His American Lovers*, my dedication reads: "Xi Jinping wanted to kill 3 million Uighurs, and you don't care; he wanted to kill 30,000 Hong Kongers, and again you don't care. Today, he is wanting to kill a million Americans. Do you still not care?"

In my prose collection, *Assassination Tutorial*, my dedication reads: "Xi Jinping established the concentration camps in Xinjiang, and you agreed; he sent the army to assassinate Hong Kongers, and again you agreed. Now that he is using the Wuhan virus to poison Americans, do you still agree? Are you an accomplice of the murderers?"

So what do I want to achieve by contacting you at this

time? —— I would like to ask you to do me a favor by kicking the current US President Trump out of the White House.

You also understand that I am not doing it for myself. I do it for the benefit of the entire American people. Of course, it can also be understood that it is for the benefit of all mankind.

You also understand that Comrade Mao Zedong's Cultural Revolution made China into a giant madhouse, but the Chinese people still love him infinitely. The situation is the same in the United States: even if President Trump has made the United States a giant madhouse, the American people will still love him infinitely.

Looking back, you can see what President Trump has done. He built a Trump wall, and as a result, he has made Congress a giant madhouse. And he launched the US-China trade war, and as a result, he has turned European countries into a giant madhouse too. He then led the US government to fight the Wuhan plague, and as a result, he has made the whole world into a giant madhouse.

And you are a senior official in the giant madhouse. So are you also a lunatic?

Don't you really feel ashamed that a great thinker like you has become a favorite in the Trump Dynasty?

So how can you help me kick President Trump out of the White House? —— I want to ask you to write a new book and publish it half a year later. Please publish it before this year's US election.

I would like to ask you to achieve the following two writing goals in your new book:

First, let the US government freeze the property of Chinese emperor Xi Jinping. The US government has frozen the properties of the dictators in Venezuela and Iran, and of course Xi Jinping's property can be frozen. As soon as the US government announces that Xi Jinping's $1 trillion assets in the United States are frozen, a coup in Beijing will immediately occur; then the CCP will perish, and peace will be restored to the world.

Second, let President Trump step down. Thus, the disaster for the American people will be over. Otherwise, the tyrant will cause many natural and humanitarian disasters. Mao Zedong had killed 150 million people in China. And this time, the shoddy work in preventing and treating the Wuhan virus will mean how many people have been killed by President Trump? It is still unknown.

If President Trump is reelected this year, the trouble for the American people will be serious. In the next two years, President Trump will definitely create more and more natural and humanitarian disasters and will kill more and more Americans.

Dictators always like to create more and more natural and humanitarian disasters and kill more and more people.

Please do me a favor to write a new book now, to save the United States.

You are the greatest thinker of our times. The title, outline, and content of your new book are up to you. I believe it will not stump you. Whatever you write, my opinion will not be wiser than yours.

Your books have been the spiritual food and the ideological weapon of all humankind. Please continue to use your power of literature, knowledge, and thought to save all humanity.

May the Lord bless you.

March 30, 2020
Washington, DC

15

I Have a Good Fight Today!

This morning, I completed the connection with Mr. Navarro. I went to the post office and mailed three of my English books to him. I want to incite him to defect and ask him to help me do one thing: kick the current US President Trump out of the White House. As long as he is willing to help me, my dream will come true.

I have always had a political desire to kick President Trump out of the White House. I don't believe that Mrs. Nancy Pelosi can do it through impeachment, or Mr. Joe Biden do it through winning the general election. I only believe in my abilities. I think that only I, through political means as such as Blossoming Campaign and Surrounding Campaign, can succeed.

Why do I always have to fight US President Trump? —— Because, last year, when the prodemocracy veteran Mr. Su Xiaokang banqueted Mr. Wang Qingying and me for dinner, he made it very clear: "In overseas prodemocracy circles, there are only two people engaged in the prodemocracy movement, Mr. Fu Xiqiu and Mr. Yang Jianli." To translate his words into the vernacular: Without the help of the United States, the Chinese democratic movement cannot succeed. The only people who can enter the US Congress and the White House to lobby are Mr. Fu and Mr. Yang. Only their actions are the most efficient.

But Mr. Su Xiaokang was talking about the situation in the past ten years. For the past three years, I have been the only one in the overseas democratic movement. Translated into the vernacular, this means: As long as President Trump does not step down, Xi Jinping will always be in power. If Trump stays in the White House for an extra minute, there will be more natural and man-made disasters, and many more people will die. Only by ousting President Trump can Xi Jinping be shot.

Therefore, in the past three years, I have been the only one who took an offensive posture and continued to attack President Trump. It was I who wrote "The Theory of the Political She-Male" and incorporated it into *Rainbow Will Rise Up*. It has been I who sent my works to President Trump and accused him of being a political she-male. Today, it is still me, asking Mr. Navarro to rebel and giving President Trump the deadliest blow.

This is the Blossoming Campaign, which is launching a political action in the center of the White House.

So is there any way I can change Navarro into a rebel? Anyway, if you can read English, just read it. I will take photos and post the letter to Navarro. I don't have much energy to teach you fools. You don't even know that as long as Trump is in power, he will continue to help Xi Jinping consolidate the monarchy. How can you overthrow the CCP? You are not fools; what are you?

If Navarro is afraid of death and dare not resist President

Trump, then I will force him to pick death; let him commit suicide by swallowing a gun.

If it is like that, the trouble will be aroused. In case he hurries and really does commit suicide in the White House, what will I do?

Instigating others to commit suicide is a criminal offence. If he dies, the FBI may arrest me and take me to court. However, the judge can also acquit me. Then I will immediately run to the home of Mr. Wei Jingsheng, the godfather of the Chinese democratic movement, to have a banquet with friends to celebrate my becoming a hero who saved the United States. His home has treasures of Wuyishan Dahongpao, a kind of tea, and Sichuan Wuliangye, a kind of white wine, which are worth tasting.

And there are other specialties in his home: the lamb meatballs boiled in cabbage soup, the tofu mixed with shallots, the steamed blue crab, the boiled fresh abalone, the garlic smashed cucumber, and the green pepper fried pork belly, among others, are all worth tasting.

But what will I do if the judge convicts me? —— Do not be afraid. By then, my bosom friends Mr. Zhao Yan and Ms. Cai Xiuling will come to the court to testify and intercede with the judge: "Please give Mr. Shisheng Chen a heavy sentence and imprison him for ten years. Let him successfully complete his doctoral degree in prison. Otherwise, if you have acquitted him in this time, he will go to work again and will have no time to study. You will waste a genius."

After ten years in jail, I will get two doctorates in prison, in Spanish literature and in mathematics. After I am released from the prison, I will immediately go to the restaurant of my bosom friend Mr. George Gao to have a banquet with friends, to celebrate my becoming a great writer in the contemporary world. His restaurant has a collection of the chrysanthemum tea of Lingyin Temple and the wines of California, which are worth tasting.

His restaurant also has some good dishes: the tofu soup with vermicelli and cabbage, the Beijing sliced duck, the braised sea cucumber, the crispy fried cod, the stir-fried bean sprouts, the moo shu pork, the beef soup of Xihu Lake, the Yangzhou fried rice, etc., all worth tasting.

At that time, I shall have two doctoral degrees, and I have used English, Spanish, and Chinese to write novels. I am not a great writer in the world, so what am I?

But hold on. Maybe it is impossible for me to go to jail for ten years. It is just I who kick President Trump out of the White House. Then, of course, the next president will be grateful and thank me for driving off the predecessor so that he can come to power. Then the new president may pardon me. Then he will summon me to the White House, award me the National Hero Medal, and thank me for saving America.

And the Royal Nobel Committee of Sweden will also thank me for saving the world and award me the Nobel Peace Prize. Then I will become a rich man. The purse of the Nobel Peace Prize is said to be one million US dollars!

Then I will immediately fly to Canada to the writer Ms. Sheng Xue's home and hold a banquet with friends to celebrate my becoming a rich man in the United States. Her house has a collection of Junshan Silver Needle, a kind of tea, and Scotch whisky, which are worth tasting.

Her home also specializes in some dishes: the soup of fish

head with tofu, the braised pork, the steamed whitebait cus-tard, the tomato fried eggs, the fermented pork knuckle, the fried potato slices, the salad of ham with corn, the leek boxes, etc., are all worth tasting .

So should I buy a few bottles of beer to drink tonight and wish to become a great hero, a great writer, and a great rich man?

April 4, 2020
Washington, DC

This is my mail bag for sending books in the post office.

These are the three English books I sent to Navarro:
Assassination Tutorial, Rainbow Will Rise Up, and
A Chinese Refugee and His American Lovers.

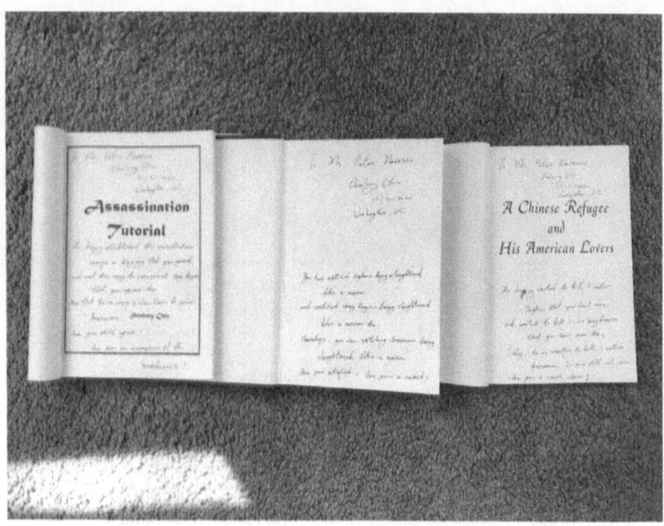

This is my inscription on the front page of
the three books I gave to Navarro.

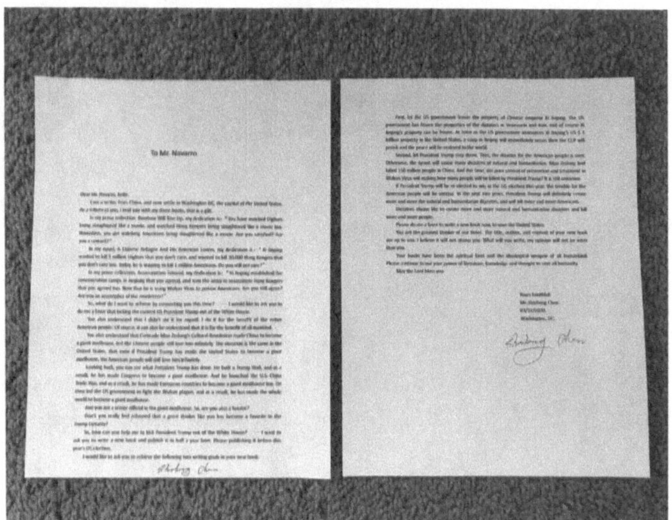

This is my letter to Mr. Navarro.

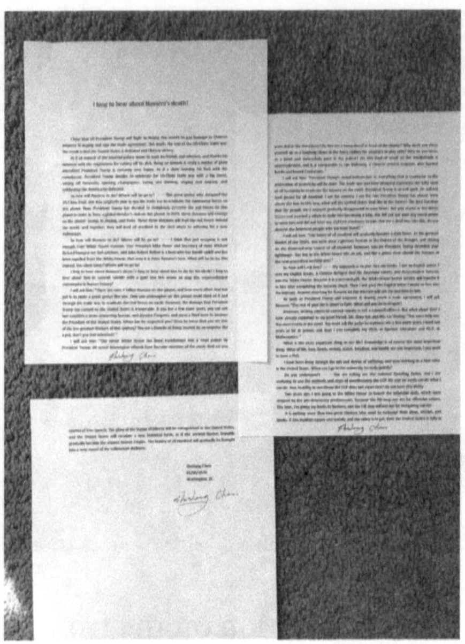

This is an article I published on the internet:
"I long to hear about Navarro's death!"

This is the post office receipt for my
books to mail to Navarro.

16

Pompeo, Are You Zhou Enlai II?

Dear Mr. Pompeo, hello.

I am a writer from China now settled in Washington, DC. This time I am giving you my three books, that, I want to ask you to help the people of the United States overcome this year's hard time. Please do not participate in the fraudulent actions of President Trump in the US election at the end of this year!

President Trump is a fool and a liar who is full of hooliganism. He has no ability to judge the right and the wrong. He does not understand what is truth and justice. Among his life beliefs, there is only such a fighting motto: Persevering until victory! —— So, how much does it cost to win? How much damage must be done in the process of winning? These, he completely ignored.

I guess that in the US elections at the end of this year, President Trump will definitely use the fraudulent means—deception, intimidation, threats, monopolies, manipulation, misleading, etc.—to be reelected the US president.

Since he has not allowed the US Congress to have a fair impeachment, how can he allow the American people to have a fair national election?

And you may become the devil's accomplice, to help President Trump get reelected.

President Trump has become a devil. According to God's theological principles, the predecessors of the devils were the angels. However, because the angels were proud, thinking that they could stand side by side with God, they became the devils. President Trump is originally a fool and a liar full of hooliganism, but because of arrogance and arbitrariness, he believes that he is a genius and a saint and the only real son of God. He thinks himself is the chosen one. Now he is trying to play God among his palms and has become a devil.

And you may be the accomplice of the devil in two possible ways. First, you are a good person by nature and always temperate and quiet, so even if you work with a devil, you can get along well. Second, you are a bad person by nature and always evil and deceitful, so even if you work with a devil, you can get along well. I would rather believe that you are the first state, so I want to ask you not to hurt the United States again and not to help President Trump to conduct the election fraud at the end of this year.

Think about it. If the United States also has election fraud, how is the United States different from Africa? The United States will be irretrievable and will perish in decay.

Just because you helped President Trump conduct election fraud this year, the United States will gradually disintegrate, fission, and perish in the next fifty years. You will have retribution. You will be without descendants!

If you do this unreasonable thing, may my curse become a reality: you will be without descendants!

Throughout the human history of the past two thousand

years, God has released the devils into the world countless times to test whether Christians faithfully obey the teachings of the Bible. God is too lazy to punish the devils and is always diligent to punish the devil's accomplices. If you assist President Trump in the fraudulent activities, you will be punished first, and then turning to your loved ones. Your loved ones will die in pain. In your later years, you will live a meaningless life, sad and distressed, in lonely agony.

Do you know that there was a founding prime minister named Zhou Enlai in China? He constantly assisted the founding emperor Mao Zedong to do evil things. Mao Zedong is a devil, and Zhou Enlai is the devil's accomplice. At that time, many founding fathers of New China were thinking the same fluke mentality: "Mao Zedong is about to kill someone's relatives, but not my relatives. Then let's kill them." Therefore, Zhou Enlai, Liu Shaoqi, Zhu De, Deng Xiaoping and other founding fathers were very keen to assist Mao Zedong in killing Chinese people. As a result, all their relatives were killed by Mao Zedong.

Are you Zhou Enlai II? Are you ready to help President Trump continue to kill the innocent American people? If you do so, it will hurt your loved ones in the end.

The tyrant's power machine is a country's crazy meat grinder, and everyone is wrapped in it, and it is impossible to escape. President Trump himself possesses the character of a tyrant. He uses the tyrant's arrogance, arbitrariness, stupidity, deception, ferocity, cruelty, coercion, and intimidation to govern the United States. Please don't help him to continue to do evil things, okay?

As a tribute to you, I mail you my three books as a gift.

In my prose collection, *Rainbow Will Rise Up*, my dedication reads: "You have watched Uighurs being slaughtered like a movie, and watched Hong Kongers being slaughtered like a movie too. Nowadays, you are watching Americans being slaughtered like a movie. Are you satisfied? Are you a coward?"

In my novel, *A Chinese Refugee and His American Lovers*, my dedication reads: "Xi Jinping wanted to kill 3 million Uighurs, and you don't care; he wanted to kill 30,000 Hong Kongers, and again you don't care. Today, he is wanting to kill a million Americans. Do you still not care?"

In my prose collection, *Assassination Tutorial*, my dedication reads: "Xi Jinping established the concentration camps in Xinjiang, and you agreed; he sent the army to assassinate Hong Kongers, and again you agreed. Now that he is using the Wuhan virus to poison Americans, do you still agree? Are you an accomplice of the murderers?"

May the Lord bless you.

April; 7, 2020
Washington, DC

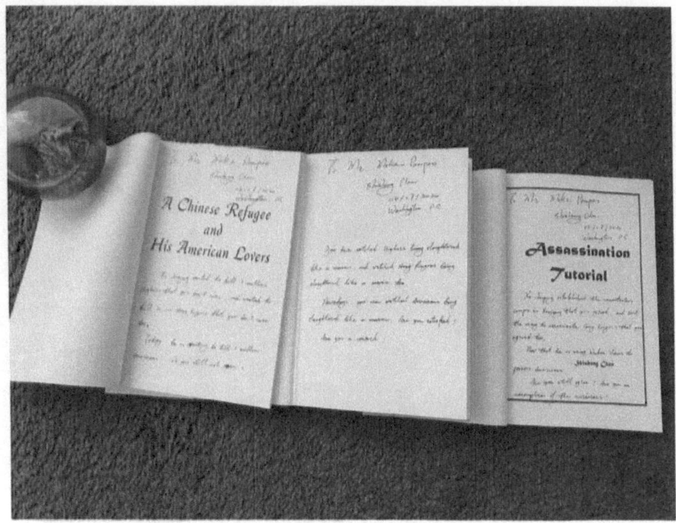

There are the title page inscriptions in my books I presented to Secretary of State Mr. Pompeo.

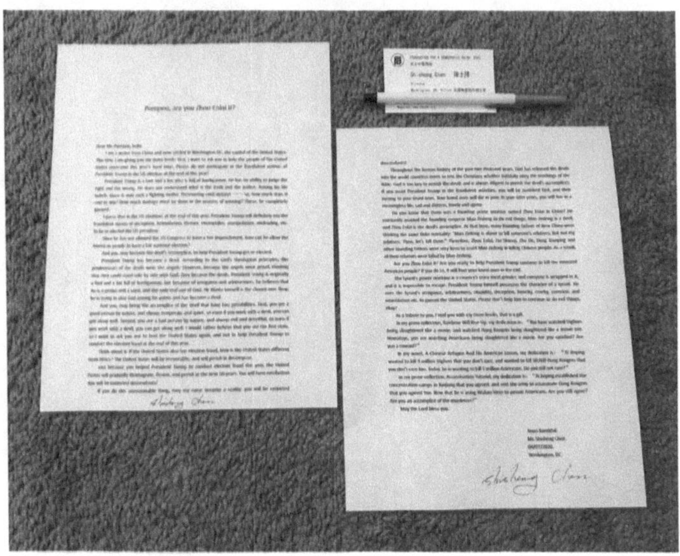

This is a letter I wrote to Secretary of State Mr. Pompeo.

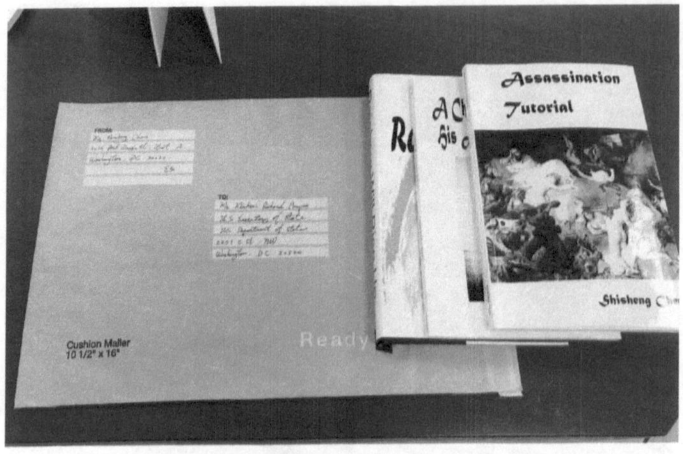

This is my mail to Secretary of State Mr. Pompeo.

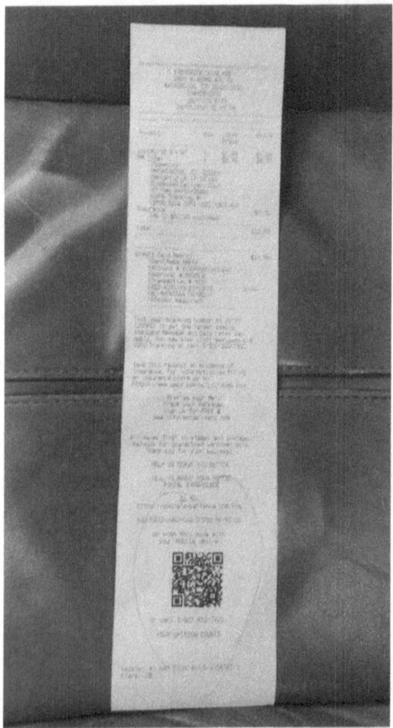

This is the mail receipt that I mailed my books
to US Secretary of State Mr. Pompeo.

These are three books I presented to Secretary of State Mr. Pompeo.

17

I Hope You All Have a Happy Death!

For two days, I was in a very depressed mood, but by yesterday, I was suddenly bright and back to normal. Because facing the result of the imminent death of the United States, I finally came up with a countermeasure.

The reason is that. The day before yesterday, US President Trump ordered the Treasury Department to print his signature on all relief checks for mailing to the victims across the United States. This means that by the end of this year, President Trump will come to life in the posture of a great anti-epidemic hero. He is the greatest hero of the contemporary era and the greatest president in American history. Without his wise leadership, the United States would have lost more than 100 million people. With his wise leadership, only less than 100,000 people died in the United States. We should shout: "Long live our great king, Trump!"

The population on the earth always completes the division like this: 10 percent of the people are sober, 10 percent are confused, and 80 percent follow suit. Those who follow the trends are always like this: whoever has the strongest propaganda, they will follow it. —— That is to say, President Trump can be reelected in 100 percent of the US elections at the end of this year.

Yes. This is a bribery election, and also a fraud. Putting President Trump's name on the relief check makes voters feel that President Trump saved them. They should of course vote for President Trump.

The incumbent president already has the advantages of election, taking advantage of the times, the geographical conditions, the presidency, and the voters. In addition, by the end of this year, President Trump will have used other means to bribe elections and fraud. Then any other presidential candidate will be at a disadvantage and find it impossible to defeat President Trump. In other words, there is no suspense for President Trump's reelection.

Yes. This is a completely unfair election, and also an unjust election. The candidate, Mr. Joe Biden, is still eager to defeat President Trump, to be a host in the White House, and heal the wounds of the United States in the coming years. This will be a wasted dream. The United States will decay day by day, and will no longer be rescued until death.

How can a gentleman defeat a ruffian? How could Biden beat Trump? President Trump will use all hooligans to win. But Biden is not a ruffian and cannot use rogue means. There is no need to fight this battle; we can judge who will win or be defeated.

President Trump ordered the Treasury Department to sign his autograph on the relief check, which is really rogue. That is to say, President Trump has no trace of confession. He doesn't even admit that he has killed 30,000 Americans who have died in the Wuhan virus plague. He has had no guilt at all. This is downright hooliganism.

The relief checks must bear the autographed name of President Trump, that is, any checks keep in the state treasury bureaus cannot be used. So the new check had to be redesigned. After the designing was completed overnight, then they were printed overnight. After the printing overnight, they were transported overnight and then flown to the airports of the various states and trucked to the treasury bureaus of the various cities where the staffs took care of mailing the checks. These steps had to slow down the relief work for at least half a month. It's really a waste of money and manpower.

For governing a large country such as the United States, these are small measures of harm. But the problem is that if President Trump resolutely seizes the presidency, the damage to the United States will become bigger and bigger. If he can be reelected this year, then he will surely be reelected for a third term in 2024. Eventually, he will restore monarchy in the United States. In this way, the disaster of the American people will follow unceasing.

Dictators always bring war, famine, poverty, plague, unrest, division, and death to the people. There is always a way of death to adapt to you. President Trump has been defeated in the US-China trade war, but you are not dead. So, no problem. But in this war against the plague of Wuhan virus, President Trump has been defeated again; now are you dead?

In the first half of this year, you passed by without dying. In the second half of this year, President Trump will forcibly lift the isolation order, allowing everyone to resume work.

Then the plague will be resurrected and break out again; now are you dead?

Even if you haven't died this year, it's okay. Two years later, the US government will be bankrupt. The United States has to borrow money from China to survive. Even if China starves 100 million people, it will lend a lot of money to the United States. Then, with the bankruptcy of the US government, your business will have closed. Will you die?

Will the US government go bankrupt? Of course. President Trump has gone bankrupt six times in his life. He knows how to bankrupt the US government. So don't panic; please enjoy the death.

Even if you have not died after two years, five years later there will be another famine in the United States. Then will you die?

Will there be famine in the United States? There have been famines in American history. Before the War of Independence, there were famines. After the War of Independence, there were famines too. The Great Depression of the United States in 1930s was the most impressive famine.

The United States is the granary of the world. American food can feed seven billion people on the planet. But will the famine also occur in the United States? Of course. In China, even during the harvest years, Chairman Mao Zedong engaged in the Great Leap Forward, which can still starve 75 million people. In Venezuela, even though the entire country is floating on a vast oil field, a nationwide famine in the past few years still caused refugees to surge into neighboring countries.

The dictators always have a way to make everyone die.

And I also face another destiny of death. At the end of this year, if President Trump is reelected, he must deliver three iron-fisted blows: to dissolve Congress, to establish a news censorship agency, and to promote McCarthyism. The most harmful to me is McCarthyism. It is a way to disguise suppression of the counterrevolutionary movement. President Trump will assassinate journalists in the movement.

Historical experience tells us that dictators must assassinate journalists in order to promote dictatorship. During the Republic of China, when the CCP assassinated journalists, that journalists en masse throughout China began to speak out against the Kuomintang and in favor of the Communist Party. Subsequently, in 1949, the CCP successfully captured China.

During the Sino-British negotiations on the future of Hong Kong, the CCP assassinated journalists, and journalists throughout Hong Kong began to promote the benefits of returning to the motherland. Subsequently, in 1997, the United Kingdom abandoned Hong Kong, and the CCP successfully captured Hong Kong.

I will never believe in any dictatorship. At the end of this year, if President Trump is reelected, I will escape from the United States in 2023 and return to France to settle.

Dear American friends, I wish you all have a happy death, to take a wonderful life from the bitterness, and to go to your heavenly home early to rest in peace with God.

Thanks be to God. Amen.

April 17, 2020
Washington, DC

18

To Mrs. Nancy Pelosi

Dear Mrs. Nancy Pelosi, hello.

I am a writer from China now settled in Washington, DC.

Since I am a Chinese prodemocracy fighter, I have attended many democratic activities in America. Therefore, in the past few years, I have been seeing you constantly. I have been most impressed twice. One time, the godfather of Chinese democratic movement, Mr. Wei Jingsheng, led me to the June 4 massacre exhibition in the US Congress that I have seen you. The pastor of China Aid, Mr. Bob Fu led me to the banquet of the Lantos Human Rights Prize, where I also saw you. However, each time I saw you, you were the speaker on stage, and I was in the audience and had no chance to talk with you.

This time, I actually want to exchange a political viewpoint with you. Since President Trump was elected as a president, the United States is dying. We can no longer stop the death of the United States. Our only wish is, in our lifetime, not to witness the death of the United States with our own eyes.

The death of the United States refers to the independence of each state and its own statehood. This is not a bad thing for the people. However, to split the United States into a European confederation with so many small nations, then as a powerful country of the world's police, the USA will be disintegrated by China. It will make us indeed sad.

But in this year's US election, President Trump will certainly be reelected. After his reelection, the Americans nightmare will continue. We may really witness the death of the United States in our own lifetime.

Why will President Trump get reelected this year? There are two reasons. First, President Trump is originally a ruffian, but Mr. Joe Biden is a gentleman. A gentleman can't fight a ruffian because the ruffian will use rogue means and the gentleman won't. President Trump will definitely cheat in the election. Therefore, President Trump will definitely be reelected.

Second, China and Russia have already firmly controlled the White House and the Senate with bribes. Whoever wins the support of China and Russia will be elected president of the United States. No US presidential candidate has enough money and enough talent to compete with the monarchs of China and Russia.

Dear Mrs. Pelosi, don't forget that you have been defeated in the two most important battles. In 2000, China firmly controlled the White House with bribes, and you firmly refused to allow China to receive MFN treatment. As a result, you have failed. In 2020, China has firmly controlled the Senate with bribes, and you firmly determined to impeach President Trump. As a result, you have failed again.

Therefore, in this year's US election, China will also firmly control the Electoral College with bribes. Mr. Joe Biden will definitely lose. The United States will be doomed to die in corruption. It will be a historic ending that cannot be changed.

Now, I just want to put a new ideological weapon into your hands, that is Shishengism. Please expose the truth in Congress: President Trump is a political she-male. His political ideals are twofold: one is to establish the Trump Dynasty nationwide, and the other is to establish a global dictators' club.

What is the political she-male? In your busy schedule, please take some time to read in my book, *Rainbow Will Rise Up*, "The Theory of Political Shemale," chapter 22.

Please use such a new ideological weapon to see whether you can kick President Trump out of the White House.

To express my respect for you, this time I present three books to you. Please take them. Thank you very much.

In my prose collection, *Rainbow Will Rise Up*, my dedication reads: "We have watched the Uyghurs being slaughtered like a tragedy, and the Hong Kongers being slaughtered like a tragedy as well. Nowadays, are we watching the Americans being slaughtered, like one more tragedy? Must we really witness the death of America in our lifetime?"

In my novel, *A Chinese Refugee and His American Lovers*, my dedication reads: "We neither stopped Xi Jinping from slaughtering 3 million Uighurs, nor stopped him from slaughtering 30,000 Hong Kongers. Nowadays, shouldn't we stop him from slaughtering a million Americans? Must we really witness the death of America in our lifetime?"

In my prose collection, *Assassination Tutorial*, my dedication reads: "Xi Jinping has established the concentration camps in Xinjiang that we have been helpless to prevent, and he has sent the army to assassinate the Hong Kongers, which we have also been helpless to stop. Nowadays, is he releasing the Wuhan pneumonia to poison the Americans, and we are still helpless? Must we really witness the death of America in our lifetime?"

May God bless you!

April 25, 2020
Washington, DC

These are my three books I presented to Mrs. Nancy Pelosi: *Rainbow Will Rise Up*, *A Chinese Refugee and His American Lovers*, and *Assassination Tutorial*.

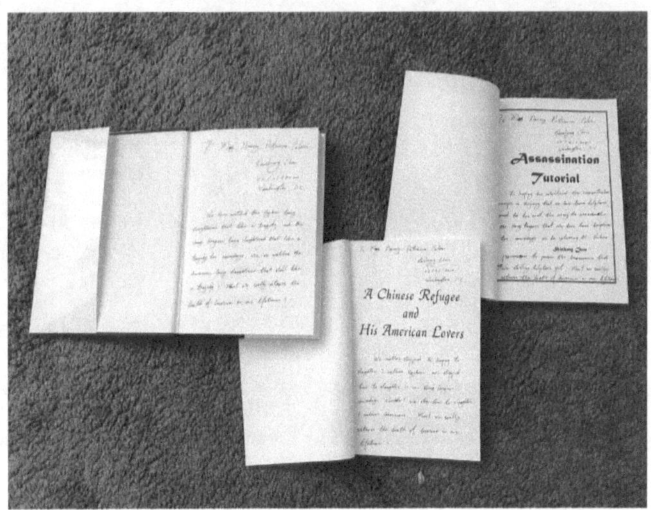

There are the inscriptions I wrote on the title pages of my three books I presented to Mrs. Nancy Pelosi.

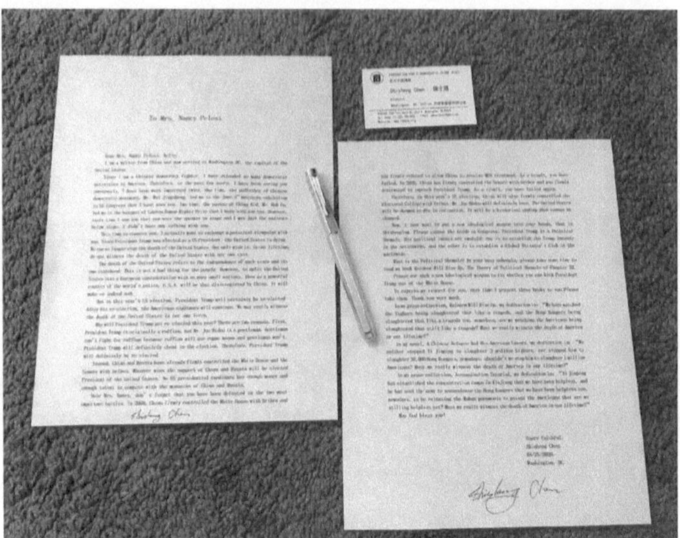

This is my English letter to Mrs. Nancy Pelosi.

This is the envelope I mailed to Mrs. Nancy Pelosi.

This is the post office receipt from my
mailing to Mrs. Nancy Pelosi.

19

Mr. Adam Schiff, the US Is Committing Suicide!

Dear Mr. Adam Schiff, hello.

I am a writer from China now settled in Washington, DC.

I've seen you. It was a few months ago, on January 30 of this year. At that time, you were debating on Capitol Hill and wanted to impeach President Trump. And I sat silently in the auditorium, quietly admiring your excellence and charm. Your tongue resembled a lotus flower blooming—bright, with a splendid fragrance. I almost worshipped you because you were like a God in the temple.

So this time I want to connect you, that is purely to want to exchange a political point of view with you: America is committing suicide!

I once wrote to Mrs. Nancy Pelosi. In the letter to her, I have laid out the death of the United States. That is, each state will be independent and build its own country. In this letter to you, I will verify America's death in detail—the mode, the route, and the timetable.

So, let me first prove the mode of America's death.

The death mode of the United States is that, because the

presidents of the United States must snatch the dog food and grab the dog shit, the United States must die.

So how does the US Presidents snatch the dog food and grab the dog shit? Let me quote directly from the description of a kind man who is a member of US House of Representatives, Mr. Chris Smith.

Last year, the Anti-Extradition Law Amendment Bill Movement of Hong Kong broke out. In order to support Hong Kong people's ideal of pursuing freedom, Chinese prodemocracy fighters established a major alliance in the United States. I am also a member of the major alliance. On September 30, 2019, under the arrangement of Pastor Bob Fu, as chairman of the China Committee of the US Congress and the Administration, Congressman Mr. Chris Smith met us on Capitol Hill. During the forty-five-minute meeting, Mr. Chris Smith spent half an hour to describe the past situation of President Clinton who snatched the dog food and grabbed the dog shit.

He told us sadly that in the past thirty years, the politicians of Washington, DC, have been subjected to contempt, ridicule, and insult by Chinese politicians, diplomats, and political brokers. He gave a historical example. On the issue of the most-favored-nation treatment to China, the unanimous decision of both the House of Representatives and the Senate believed that China should not be granted the most-favored-nation treatment. Who knew, the Chinese were all in unison with full of confidence, and laughed loudly at the members of US Congress: "We will get the most-favored-nation treatment!"

Sure enough, on a public holiday, when members of both

the House of Representatives and the Senate went home for a break, President Clinton suddenly signed an order granting China's most-favored-nation treatment one night before leaving office.

This shows what? This shows that in the past thirty years, members of the US Senate and House of Representatives have been bullied by Chinese officials. The American presidents are shameless and unwilling to protect the dignity of the American legislators.

This shows what? This shows that in the past thirty years, the butt of every American president has been shit. They play around with the US Congressmen.

This shows what? This shows that in the past 30 years, the Presidents of the United States have been the corrupt elements and the criminal elements.

When the United States is already dominated by corrupt elements and criminals, how could the United States not go to ruin?

The scene where Congressman Mr. Chris Smith met us on the day was preserved on site. Everyone can testify.

On that day, the prodemocracy fighters who attended the meeting included many famous figures: Mr. Zhao Xin, Ms. Jin Xiuhong, Mr. Chen Weiming, Ms. Xiang Li, Mr. Zhao Changqing, Mr. Guo Baosheng, Mr. Jin Chang, Mrs. Zuo Haiyan, Ms. Zheng Yun, Ms. Li Yeqing, Mr. Bai Mingxin, Mr. Ding Jianqiang, Mr. Wang Kaiming, Mr. Felipe Alexandre, Ms. Lise King, Ms. Elizabeth Hilyard, and others. They all witnessed Mr. Chris Smith's description: President Clinton snatched the dog food and grabbed the dog shit.

This is the death mode of the United States.

Dear Mr. Adam Schiff, now let me describe about the death route of the United States.

There are two death routes for the United States. One way leads to acute suicide, which will make America die immediately within fifty years. Another way amounts to chronic suicide, that it will make America slowly dying after fifty years to five hundred years.

The situation of acute suicide will copy the route of the state suicide of the ancient China. More than two thousand years ago, during the Spring and Autumn Period and the Warring States Period, Qin state could never defeat the powerful Chu state. So Qin state sent lobbyist Zhang Yi to bribe Chu state. When the king of Chu state's favorite concubine, Zheng Xiu, received the money, she expelled the nobleman Qu Yuan. In 278 BC, the great poet Qu Yuan committed suicide. Then, the ruling class of Chu state was completely bought by Qin state and gradually went to extinction.

At that time, did not the nobles of Chu state know that accepting the enemy state's money was selling their own state? And that betrayal would eventually destroy their own state, and eventually, they would be killed by the enemy? —— At that time, the nobles of Chu state all knew that they would die. "However, money must be collected, since our king is so rich, but he is not afraid of death. We nobles, who have no money, why are we afraid of death?"

This is an overview of American politics today. All US presidents and some US senators are collecting Chinese money. All the bribe takers know that accepting the money of the enemy country is the act of betraying their own country. And betrayal of their own country will eventually make the United

States perish. Eventually, we may also go to prison. —— But money must be collected. Since the presidents of the United States are so rich, they are not afraid of death. We senators are so poor, why are we afraid of death?

Snatching dog food and grabbing dog shit eventually will bring the United States to be destroyed within fifty years.

The situation of chronic suicide of the United States will copy the suicide of the ancient Roman Republic. More than two thousand years ago, the ancient Roman Republic gradually evolved into the ancient Roman Empire, and its chronic suicide experienced three political shock waves.

The first political shock wave was that in 82 BC, Lucius Cornelius Sulla led his army to occupy Rome, setting a precedent for military dictatorship, and had himself appointed the lifelong dictator.

The second political shock wave was that in 60 BC, Marcus Licinius Crassus, Gaius Julius Caesar, and Gnaeus Pompey formed a secret alliance to become the first three-headed alliance.

The third political shock wave was that in 43 BC, Mark Antony, Marcus Aemilius Lepidus, and Gaius Octavius Augustus formed an open alliance to become the last three-headed alliance.

In the end, Octavius won the honor of Augustus, became the founding father, and restored the monarchy.

At present, President Trump is only the first political shock wave in the United States. He is like Lucius Cornelius Sulla, and is preparing to establish a dictatorship. But President Trump's dictatorship is doomed to failure because the American people are psychologically unprepared and unwilling to accept dictatorship.

After President Trump disappears in the political arena of the United States, the presidents to be elected later are each more corrupt and worse than the past. Slowly, the people will begin to lose patience and gradually become numb. Everyone knows that this country is hopelessly going to restore the monarchy. Well, let it be. As a result, the United States will copy the history from the Roman Republic to the Roman Empire and from the democratic to the dictatorial.

This is the death route for the United States.

Dear Mr. Adam Schiff, now let me describe about the death timetable of the United States.

In fact, there is little to say about the death schedule of the United States. In general, the following two predictions will occur.

First, if President Trump is reelected this year, the United States will embark on the path of acute suicide. Within fifty years, the United States will be dead, and each state will become independent to found its own country.

Perhaps, in our lifetime, we may witness the disintegration of the United States.

Second, if President Trump loses the election this year, the United States will still embark on the path of chronic suicide. After fifty years but within five hundred years, the United States will be dead, and each state will become independent to found its own country.

However, the chronic death of the United States is not a matter that needs consideration. The long years to come in future do not require the attention of the politicians of our times. Maybe there will be a great hero then who will change the trajectory of history? Therefore, we do not need to think too remotely.

In other words, our immediate responsibility is to let President Trump lose his election this year. As long as he is no longer reelected, the United States will not continue on the road to suicide.

You have longed for American young people to join American politics, just like the young people in European countries such as Denmark and the Netherlands. That is a thing that will never happen. American politicians are snatching dog food and grabbing dog shit in American politics. How can young people be allowed to share the dog food and the dog shit?

So how to make President Trump lose this year? Please spread Shishengism in the US Congress. Please tell every member of Congress that President Trump is a political she-male. President Trump has two political ideals. The first is to establish the Trump Dynasty in the United States, and the second is to establish a global dictators' club around the world.

What is a political she-male? Please take a look at chapter 22, "The Theory of the Political She-Male," in my book *Rainbow Will Rise Up.*

The theory of the political she-male is an ideological weapon. I hope that after you have this ideological weapon, you can defeat President Trump.

To express my respect for you, at this time I present three books to you. Please keep them. Thank you very much.

In my prose collection, *Rainbow Will Rise Up*, my dedication reads: "We have watched the Uyghurs being slaughtered like a tragedy, and the Hong Kongers being slaughtered, like another tragedy. Nowadays, are we watching the Americans being slaughtered, like yet another tragedy? Must we really witness the death of America in our lifetime?"

In my novel, *A Chinese Refugee and His American Lovers*, my dedication reads: "We neither stopped Xi Jinping from slaughtering 3 million Uighurs, nor stopped him from slaughtering 30,000 Hong Kongers. Nowadays, shouldn't we stop him from slaughter a million Americans? Must we really witness the death of America in our lifetime?"

In my prose collection, *Assassination Tutorial*, my dedication reads: "Xi Jinping has established the concentration camps in Xinjiang that we have been helpless to prevent, and he has sent the army to assassinate the Hong Kongers, which we have also been helpless to prevent. Nowadays, is he releasing the Wuhan pneumonia to poison the Americans, and are we still helpless? Must we really witness the death of America in our lifetime?"

May God bless you!

May 5, 2020
Washington, DC

These are the three books I presented to US Congressman Mr. Adam Schiff, *Assassination Tutorial*, *A Chinese Refugee and His American Lovers*, and *Rainbow Will Rise Up*.

There are my inscriptions in my three books that I presented to US Representative Mr. Adam Schiff.

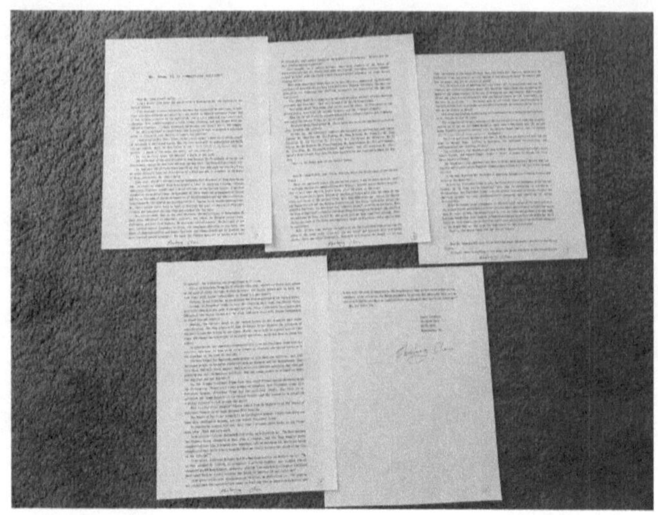

This is my letter to US Representative Mr. Adam Schiff.

This is the envelope in which I mailed my books
to US Representative Mr. Adam Schiff.

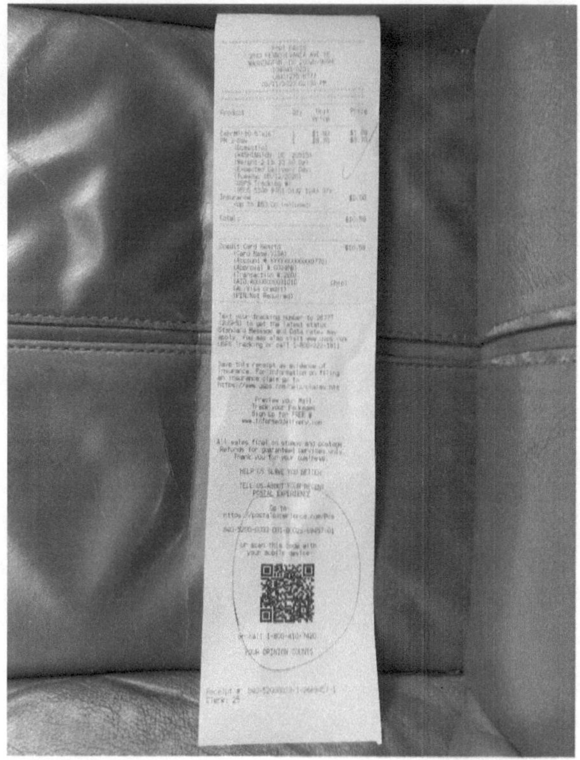

This is the post office receipt from mailing my books to US Representative Mr. Adam Schiff.

20

Mr. Chris Smith, the Shit-Eating Emperor Is Here!

Dear Mr. Chris Smith, hello.

I am a writer from China now settled in Washington, DC.

My condo is very close to Congress. I often go to Congress for Chinese democracy activities. Therefore, I have seen you many times in Congress. You have always been the chief sitting on the rostrum, and I have always been in the audience in front of the stage.

But I have twice had face-to-face conversations with you. The first time was the summer of the previous year. Mr. Qin Jin and Ms. Sheng Xue, the chairman and chairwoman of Federation for a Democratic China (FDC), took me to meet you in the US Congress, and I exchanged a few words with you. The second time was last fall, when Ms. Jin Xiuhong, known as Jane, the chairwoman of the US branch of Federation for a Democratic China (FDC), took me to meet you in the US Congress, and we talked briefly.

Okay, less gossip, come back to business. I connect with you now because I actually want to ask you to consider using a new method to save the United States. It is a method I call Shishengism.

What is Shishengism? —— This is a new political theory and a new ideological weapon. Such a political theory and ideological weapon have never appeared in human history. I am working to concentrate this political theory and this ideological weapon into my two books, *Rainbow Will Rise Up* and *How to Destroy America*. *Rainbow Will Rise Up* was published early this year. The Chinese version of *How to Destroy America* will be published next month, and the English version will be published three months later.

In the final analysis, Shishengism's doctrine recounts a simple principle: Mr. Trump, the current president of the United States, is a political she-male and a shit-eating emperor. He has two political ideals. The first is to establish the Trump Dynasty in the United States, and the second is to establish a global dictators' club around the world. Because he wants to achieve his evil political goals, he is the public enemy of all humankind. We must use any political means to destroy him for the sake of justice!

Therefore, I want to mentally destroy him, humiliate him, and defeat him, and prevent him from being reelected as president of the United States in 2025 and becoming the first emperor in American history.

You may be laughing at me: "Unless the American people are all blind. Otherwise, President Trump will definitely not be able to win the election this year." —— No! You can laugh at me. But the question is, if President Trump is really reelected at the end of this year, do you have any way to expel him from the White House?

Therefore, my actions lay the groundwork for this. *Rainbow Will Rise Up* and *How to Destroy America* seem to be two time bombs, which may explode at any time in the future. President Trump can restore the monarchy, and you cannot stop him. However, my two books can stop him at any time in the years to come.

Please promote Shishengism in the US Congress. Please spread this kind of political theory. Please distribute this kind of ideological weapon. Please arm every member of Congress to resist the dark rule of President Trump.

So what is a political she-male? Please take a look at Chapter 22, "The Theory of the Political She-Male," in *Rainbow Will Rise Up*.

Political she-male theory is an ideological weapon. I hope that after you have this ideological weapon, you will be able to defeat President Trump.

So what is a shit-eating emperor? Please read my article, "The Technology of Making the Dragon-Gold Pill," which I have attached for you.

In ancient China, human feces was used as medicine. Therefore, some Chinese people can treat sickness by eating feces. *Compendium of Materia Medica* is a huge medical book in ancient China, which written by the great medical scientist Mr. Li Shizhen of the Ming Dynasty. It contains everything, and it is introduced that all substances of nature can be used as medicine. All animal shit can be used for pharmaceuticals. Therefore, the use of human feces for pharmaceutical production is a major medical achievement. It is scientific.

However, the use of human feces for pharmaceuticals had not been mass-produced in China. Everything was based on the diagnosis experience of individual doctors, and it was carried out clinically.

However, can eating shit really cure disease? Is it really a scientific behavior? —— It is really a scientific behavior. In the 1970s, a medical document recorded such an event. A Chinese general suffered from severe stomach problems and was dying. The doctor responsible for treating him secretly collected the feces of a healthy man and made it into a capsule. He said that this was a new stomach medicine and tricked the general into taking the medicine orally. In fact, the general's stomach was lacking a bacterium that helps digestion, and that bacterium was in the feces of the healthy man. As a result, the doctor successfully cured the general's stomach.

Therefore, using human feces to treat diseases is actually a scientific behavior.

But only a kind of health-care medicine made in the legends of Qing Dynasty—the Dragon-Gold Pill—is a religious act. It can be taken arbitrarily regardless of any gender and any age.

It is nontoxic, and it will not harm the body if eaten. But because it is made of shit by the emperor, eating it will make everyone feel refreshed and energetic, with the blessing and glory of the emperor!

Today, our Chinese people universally call President Trump the shit-eating president on the internet. This is because President Trump has listened to and followed all the lies of the Chinese emperor Xi Jinping. In other words, he is eating the shit from Xi Jinping. On the spiritual range, he is eating the Dragon-Gold Pill.

So how to make the Dragon-Gold Pill? —— I have appended an article, "The Technology of Making the Dragon-Gold Pill," and you can read it when you are free, and use it as a leisure reading to increase your knowledge.

The Dragon-Gold Pill has actually existed in Chinese history, but it has never entered the stage of mass production. It's just an occasional production of the royal pharmacy. I have researched out its entire production process and written this historical paper. It is of course also a scientific paper.

And President Trump is indeed a shit-eating emperor. I hope you can understand it.

Dear Mr. Chris, to express my respect for you, at this time I present three books to you. Please keep them. Thank you very much.

In my prose collection, *Rainbow Will Rise Up*, my dedication reads: "We have watched Uyghurs being slaughtered like a tragedy, and Hong Kongers being slaughtered like another tragedy. Nowadays, are we watching Americans being slaughtered, like still another tragedy? Must we really witness the death of America in our lifetime?"

In my novel, *A Chinese Refugee and His American Lovers*, my dedication reads: "We neither stopped Xi Jinping from slaughtering 3 million Uighurs, nor stopped him from slaughtering 30,000 Hong Kongers. Nowadays, shouldn't we stop him from slaughtering a million Americans? Must we really witness the death of America in our lifetime?"

In my prose collection, *Assassination Tutorial*, my dedication reads: "Xi Jinping has established the concentration camps in Xinjiang that we have been helpless to stop, and he has sent the army to assassinate Hong Kongers, which we have also been helpless to stop. Nowadays, is he releasing the Wuhan pneumonia to poison Americans; are we still helpless to stop this? Must we really witness the death of America in our lifetime?"

May God bless you!

May 29, 2020
Washington, DC

These are my three books that I presented to Mr. Chris, *Rainbow Will Rise Up*, *Assassination Tutorial*, and *A Chinese Refugee and His American Lovers*.

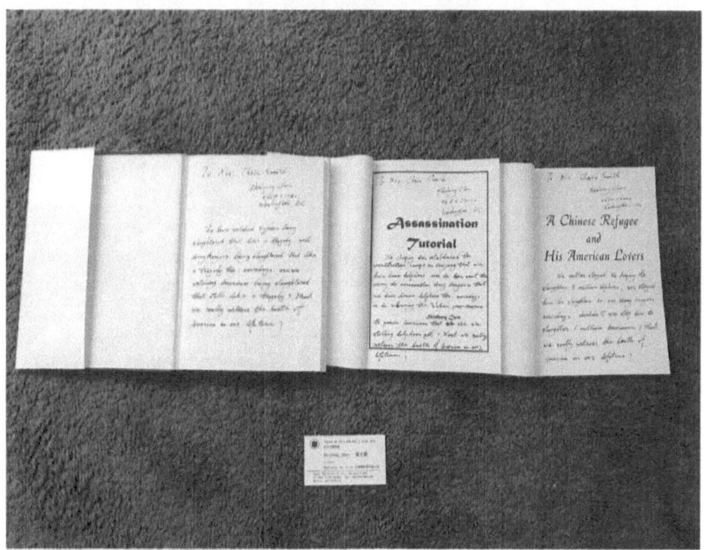

I wrote inscriptions in my three books.

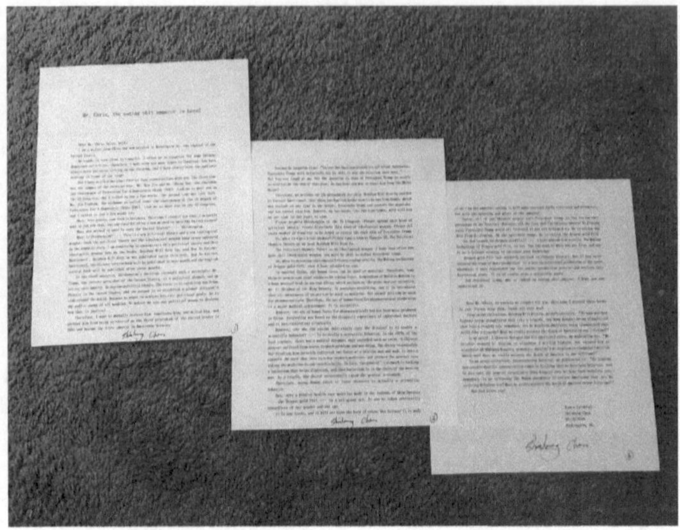

This is my letter to Mr. Chris.

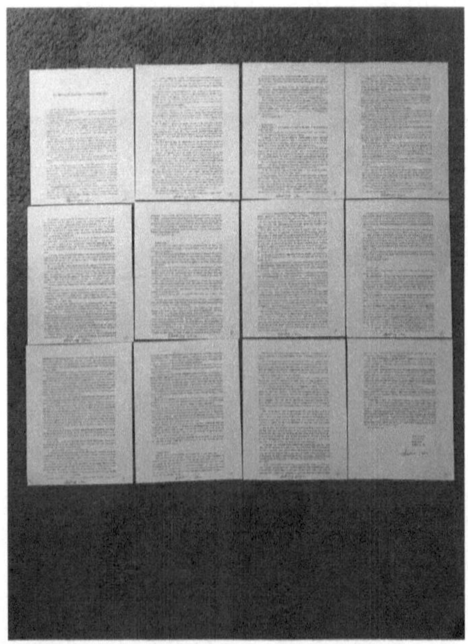

This is my appendix article to Mr. Chris, "The Technology of Making the Dragon-Gold Pill."

This is the package I mailed to Mr. Chris.

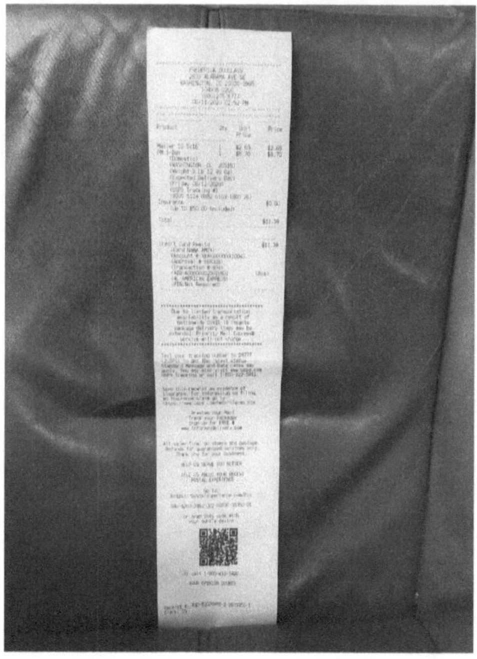

This is the mailing receipt from the post office.

21

The Technology of Making
the Dragon-Gold Pill

Dear Mr. Chris Smith, hello.

Now, I want to share with you a mysterious herbal knowledge that belongs to the Orient: the technology of making the Dragon-Gold Pill. —— Just relax, and please read this letter as a casual reading.

In ancient China, the emperor was the incarnation of the real dragon from heaven. The emperor was not a human, but a dragon. The emperor was the son of God, and he ruled the country on behalf of God. The emperor was the incarnation of God.

Therefore, in order to flatter the emperor, the royal literati respected the emperor's body, face, shit, urine, farts, and saliva as the dragon-body, the dragon-face, the dragon-gold, the dragon-water, the dragon-song, and the dragon-honeydew.

The emperor was the country. The entire Chinese people revolved around the emperor. Everyone missed the emperor very much. However, the emperor couldn't meet everyone in all of China. Therefore, the market created such a demand that everything the emperor touched was a sacred object and should be worshipped day and night.

In this way, the market had promoted a demand: Can the emperor's shit be given to everyone? It was so wasteful to throw away the emperor's shit. —— In this way, the craft of making the Dragon-Gold Pill came into being.

The emperor's shit was sacred shit. This piece of shit was used to worship; how wonderful! So how to turn it into a fragrant offering to be enshrined in the incense table? Or after worshipping this piece of shit, how to distribute it to relatives and friends, so they may take it into their bellies and always remember the grace of our emperor? Was that not even better?

Our emperor is originally a long-lived man in the eyes of the Chinese people. The emperor is a god and should live ten thousand years. In this way, we the courtiers, who can eat the shit of God, will surely live to be one thousand years old! We must eat shit so that we can get the emperor's glory and blessing.

In this way, the function of the Dragon-Gold Pill was changed from offering to tasting. The Chinese people must eat this piece of shit.

The demand in many markets was actually selling a lifestyle, culture, and concept of living. For example, there are flower shops all over the world; in Japan, in Thailand, and in China, there are different flower arrangements, but these products are actually boring. Only when it becomes a lifestyle, culture, and concept of living does it become a market.

Take another example, the diamond. Two hundred years ago, humans did not want this useless stone at all. But when some businessmen endowed it with the faithfulness of love, it represented a special lifestyle, culture, and concept. Then it became sacred, chaste, and solemn. Since then, it has become extremely noble, holy, and precious.

Qingfeng Pharmacy in Beijing had been the royal drug-store of the Qing Dynasty since three hundred years ago, and it was dedicated to the royal medicine. Because of their frequent visited to the emperor's bed, the royal doctors often had to be in touch with the emperor's shit and urine. One day, the royal doctors decided that they must take the emperor's shit out of the royal palace and use it to make the Dragon-Gold Pill to supply the marketing demand.

In the huge Forbidden City, there was no toilet. Everyone's shit was collected in the wood trucks, and it was transported out of the palace from Anding Gate three times a month. The fourth, the fourteenth, and the twenty-fourth days of the lunar calendar were the days of the manure transportation. At that time, there were a lot of wood trucks to transport away the shit and urine of the 30,000 residents living in the Forbidden City.

But the emperor's shit was the greatest treasure in the world, and it would be dealt with separately. On the day of the manure transport, the emperor's internal eunuch personally carried a carved sandalwood toilet to Anding Gate and handed it to a Qingfeng Pharmacy representative. Three times a month, Qingfeng Pharmacy must have someone standing outside the Anding Gate, personally waiting for a eunuch to send the emperor's shit, and then take it back to Qingfeng Pharmacy for product pharmaceuticals.

Generally speaking, when the emperor was ill, his shit could not be used as medicine and was dumped. When the emperor had diarrhea, his shit was sparse, and it was not easy to store, so it had to be dumped too. Only when the emperor was in good health did his shit fall down as a treasure worthy of cherishing.

However, the emperor lived in the palace and was always tortured by the love of 10,000 court ladies. Therefore, the emperor was sick most of the time, and his good-looking shit was always a scarce product in the world, and not enough could be provided to the public. That was to say, the emperor's anus often couldn't make good shit, and the amount of shit he contributed to the public was insufficient.

This caused led to a scarcity of the Dragon-Gold Pill. Generally speaking, every day the emperor's good shit was kept and the bad shit was thrown away. One barrel was collected every ten days. Each bucket of emperor's shit capacity was enough to make ten capsules of Dragon-Gold Pills. The amount of emperor's shit for one month was enough to make thirty capsules of Dragon-Gold Pills. The sales of Dragon-Gold Pills were also determined in this way. There was no single retail supply, and only one-time wholesale was provided. If customers wanted to buy, every time they must go to Qingfeng Pharmacy to buy thirty capsules, the price was 3000 taels of silver.

One capsule of Dragon-Gold Pill was one hundred taels of silver.

One hundred taels of silver could buy a common house in Qing Dynasty.

The high price limited consumers' access. The traffickers and the grassroots simply could not afford such expensive luxury goods. So it must be the royal nobles, the wealthy merchants, and the high-ranking officials who could buy the Dragon-Gold Pill.

And profits were distributed in this way. Every time the eunuch sent the emperor's shit, he received a reward of one hundred taels of silver. Thus, the eunuchs could receive three hundred taels of silver each month. And then the emperor's several inner eunuchs shared the money in every month.

The remaining profits would be exclusively gotten by Qingfeng Pharmacy.

Well, everyone knew this shit was excreted from the emperor's ass. How did it become a medicine? How did it become a health care product in life? How did it become a luxury product in the market? How did it become a fashionable element of lifestyle, a culture of communication, and a concept of livelihood? Later, how did it become a religious worship ritual? —— Next, I will reveal its craftsmanship and let you know more.

Now that Qingfeng Pharmacy had collected the emperor's shit, the workers would start the first pharmaceutical process: drying.

In general, a piece of shit was spread on a bamboo dustpan, and it took seven days of exposure to dry it completely. However, the weather in Beijing is sometimes continuously rainy days or snowy days, and there is no sun at all. Then it must be spread on a frying pan and slowly dried with charcoal fire.

In the process of drying shit, the flies would be attracted. Flies would make maggots come out of this pile of shit. It didn't matter. Switzerland has a similar method of making cheese. It is exposed to the open air, and the flies are attracted to it to produce maggots. The Swiss cut it into small pieces and eat them with the live maggots. They say: "This is the most delicious country cheese in the world."

But even if the Dragon-Gold Pill was born with maggots, people could not eat live maggots. In the process of exposure, the maggots also died. It just increased the protein content of the Dragon-Gold Pill, making it even more delicious.

The shit after drying was squeezed by hand and spread into powder. At this time, it would not have the slightest smell.

I have traveled to Tibet. I've seen Tibetans collect cattle shit in the wild, stir it with water, and squeeze it into wet clumps and shoot them on the walls outside. After the sun dries it, the cattle shit becomes a good firewood. At that time, using them to boil water for cooking, this fuel will emit a slight fragrance to drive off the cold and dehumidify and warms a space nicely.

After drying the emperor's shit, the workers stored it in the attic. When the next shipment of shit arrived, it was dried and stored. After the three monthly loads were dried, the second pharmaceutical process was started: crushing.

Cinnamon, lily, poria, astragali, licorice, pseudo-ginseng, tangerine, gastrodia, and other traditional Chinese medicines were all medicinal herbs for relieving the cold, dehumidifying, nourishing the body, reducing phlegm, preventing cough, and diffusing fragrance. These traditional Chinese medicines could be used as the auxiliary materials for making the Dragon-Gold Pill. Still, the emperor's shit was the main material of the Dragon-Gold Pill.

The auxiliary materials were subdivided into three processes and crushed. First an iron knife was used to cut all the herbs into small pieces. Then the medicinal materials were poured into a small copper bowl and smashed with a copper hammer. Then all the medicinal materials were poured into a large iron boat-shaped milling trough, where an iron wheel was used to crush it into granules.

Then the third pharmaceutical process was started: grinding.

Auxiliary materials were crushed into the granules, and then all were mixed together and poured into a mortar made of granite. Then all was ground with a granite pestle into powder.

A total of thirty Dragon-Gold Pills can be made in one grinding, to conserve the resources of manpower, material, and salary.

The pile of shit after grinding began to radiate mesmerizing fragrances of herbs and spices, and it could make everyone salivate.

At this time, it was no longer a pile of shit but a pile of powder. It could be said to be a spice for cooking and a medicine for curing diseases. However, it was still not possible to eat at that time. It was time to start the next pharmaceutical process: boiling.

This powdered shit could not be sold to customers because of poor taste and poor appearance. Thus, in order to increase its taste and appearance, it must be boiled into a paste for ease of carrying. So workers picked the cores out of red dates and hawthorn fruits, cut them into pieces, minced them, added honey and donkey-hide gelatin, put them in a wok, stirred to fry slowly, added water, stirred constantly, and simmered it into a paste.

Then, the paste was put into a wooden steamer, which was

then attached to an iron tripod. The tripod was put on top of the cooking stove, to boil the paste until well done.

The next pharmaceutical process was: pilling.

Next, they shoveled the steaming paste out of the steamer with a small iron shovel, and then pressed the paste into a round wooden mold. After cooling a little, they dug it out with a wood scraper and spread it on the table. By this time, it had turned into pills that were slightly sticky and warm, so one by one they were rubbed by hand into round pills.

At this point, the Dragon-Gold Pill was basically made. The next step was to solve a series of problems it encountered. How to store it? How to carry it? How to eat it? —— Thus, the production process of Dragon-gold Pill was divided into the production of the dry goods and the wet goods.

The dry goods, also called the coated pill, were used for cooking. It was also sometimes used for soaking in alcohol. The cooking method was to add medicinal wine, vinegar, and ginger juice into the glutinous rice flour and heat it with an iron pan to make a paste. Then, in another iron pan, the Dragon-Gold Pill paste was sprinkled with cinnabar powder and rubbed a few times. In this way, a layer of the cinnabar powder was firmly adhered into the surface of the Dragon-Gold Pill, which became extremely cute.

Then the Dragon-Gold Pill was sent to the attic to dry. The whole process lasted a month until all the moisture was evaporated. In this way, it could completely prevent insects, borers, mildew, and moisture, without changing the smell. They must be dried in a cool place. If they were exposed under the sun or dried on the stove, whole pills would be cracked, marring their appearance.

In this way, the Dragon-Gold Pill had changed from a black sticky paste into a red hard pill. It was looked bright, rosy, and lovely. By this time, no one would think that it was the emperor's shit and had been smelly. By this time, it was so cute that everyone just wanted to eat it.

But it was too hard, there was no water at all, and teeth could not bite it. If you swallowed it, you would have indigestion. So you could eat it this way: Use a mortar to crush it into a powder. Then tear crabs apart and sprinkle the powdered Dragon-Gold Pill onto the crab shells and crab meats. Then it was sprinkled with salt and peanut oil, adding onion, ginger, and white wine, after which it was steamed. Then the crab meat was eaten with seasoning from a small dish of soy sauce and sesame oil. This was actually a very wonderful dish.

This was a famous dish. Dragon-Gold Pill was essentially a wonderful spice for cooking.

The wet goods, also called the honey pill, were used for the mouth food. It didn't need to be exposed to the sun or coated with cinnabar. These black pills were directly sealed into wax balls to be made into the wax pill. When someone needs to eat it, tear the wax ball, take out the Dragon-Gold Pill, and eat it with water, tea, or white wine.

At that time, the honey remained intact in the Dragon-Gold Pill, and it melted easily in the mouth. Even the elderly without teeth could eat it and swallow it.

Chenliji Pharmacy in Guangzhou is a Chinese medicine shop established more than four hundred years ago. It is identified by the Guinness Book of Records as the oldest pharmaceutical factory still operating in the world. It invented the wax pill to store traditional Chinese medicine products more than four hundred years ago. This is an epoch-making milestone, which marks the leap forward of Chinese pharmaceutical product from soup production to pill production.

Enclosing medicinal products in a wax pill can indeed achieve the effect of preventing insects, borers, mildew, and moisture, and will not change the taste. It is more convenient to carry, transport, store, and consume.

Qingfeng Pharmacy in Beijing also created a wax-pill room as a workshop when making the Dragon-Gold Pill. The wax-pill production technology was fully popularized throughout the Qing Dynasty, and all provincial pharmacies had their own wax-pill workshops. Qingfeng Pharmacy learned the wax-pill technology of Chenliji Pharmacy.

The problem of the Dragon-Gold Pill's taste had been solved, and the problem of its appearance had been solved too. The last process was: packaging.

Only with good packaging could good sales be realized. The Dragon-Gold Pill sold so expensively that it had to rely on packaging. In the next section, I will tell you how Qingfeng Pharmacy packed the Dragon-Gold Pill.

Packaging the Dragon-Gold Pill involved five processes.

The first process was to wrap the Dragon-Gold Pill with a yellow paper. This process was limited to the dry goods. Because the coated good was attached to cinnabar, it easily dyed the silk red, and it looked very unsightly. However, if it was a wet product, the wax-pill itself would not adhere to any color, so this process could be omitted.

The second process was that a piece of yellow silk embroidered with a dragon was used to wrap up thirty Dragon-Gold Pills. In ancient China, the yellow silk was an imperial object color and used exclusively by the emperor, and others were not allowed to use it. As soon as it appeared, it would remind Chinese people of the dignity and sacredness of the emperor.

Many folk items could use yellow silk to embroider a dragon, but they must be related to the religious themed items before they could be used. And the Dragon-Gold Pill was essentially used for worship, and it was also regarded as a religious item.

The third process was that it was then wrapped with an oil paper to achieve the purpose of preventing moisture.

The fourth process was that it was loaded into a silver box to make it look precious.

The fifth process was that, finally, the silver box was put into a carved sandalwood box, and the wooden cover of the box was inlaid with some auspicious pictures with shells. In this way, it looked more solemn.

In this way, the whole Dragon-Gold Pill's box exuded a slight fragrance. Customers who bought it were reluctant to eat the pills immediately and always wanted to put it on the altar to burn incense to worship for one year.

After all, Qingfeng Pharmacy made Dragon-Gold Pill once a month with a limited production of thirty capsules each time. A total of twelve boxes of Dragon-Gold Pill were sold in limited quantities each year. The things were rare. But on the market, it was not for the highest bidder; not everyone could buy it. Even if the price was high, sales depended on the identity of the customers. Qingfeng Pharmacy was an old brand that paid attention to credibility and medical ethics and was not short of money. It would not make fakes for money to ruin its reputation as an old pharmacy.

In this regard, the Dragon-Gold Pill had become a good gift. Some governors of the Qing Dynasty specifically sent retinues to Qingfeng Pharmacy in Beijing to buy the Dragon-Gold Pill. There were also some lower-level officials who, in order to be promoted to buy the Dragon-Gold Pill, bribed higher-level officials. Of course, there were also some high-ranking officials who, during the festival, used the Dragon-Gold Pill as a gift to friends and relatives.

Every foodie knew that this thing was made of emperor's shit, but it was completely harmless to the human body. If someone ate the Taoist drug, there were often reports of dead people. The alchemy medicines, which contained lead, mercury, and quicksilver, could cause poisoning and death. But the Dragon-Gold Pill had never reported a dead person. It was shit excreted from the emperor's body. If we might be about to die, the emperor would die first. The emperor was our drug tester. Therefore, eating it was completely harmless.

So many foodies ate it out of curiosity. After all, life is full of flavor. Every taste of life should be tasted in order to fully live this life.

For the sake of good health, compared with the two, should I eat Taoist elixir or eat imperial Dragon-Gold Pill? The rich, of course, were more willing to eat Dragon-Gold Pill.

Who knew this taste would be eaten, and a lifestyle would be formed? It became popular and well-known. Whether it was the dry goods—the coated pills for cooking dishes that were delicious—or the wet goods, the honey pills to be accompanied by meals with fine wine—it was also extremely delicious.

In the Zen room where sandalwood was burned, a rich

man lay on the Arhat bed, chewing Dragon-Gold Pill in the dim candlelight, consuming the opium, closing his eyes and raising his mind, and thinking about what possible paradise will be in front of his eyes. In a surreal fluttering, he dreamed of one day ascending into a royal palace to be a king, sitting on the throne and facing dozens of ministers kneeling at his feet, trembling, crying, and begging him to spare their lives.

The feeling of being a god is really good! When I thought of the ten thousand beautiful women in the harem, always looking forward to my bestowing favors on them! So why should I still care about what these lowly ministers do at my feet? I'll kill them if I want to. Let's kill a few first, and then hurry back to the harem, holding the two amazing legs of my concubine, and playing with her three-inch soles. Then ask the big tits nurse to bring a bowl of human milk and feed me slow sips. This is so wonderful to me!

This is the magical use of the Dragon-Gold Pill. If someone can't eat the shit produced by the emperor's ass, where to get such a pleasant sexual fantasy?

It seems in modern society that a fetishist is always collecting women's underwear, stockings, bras, lipstick, high heels, perfumes, and other female items, and then secretly putting them out on his bed with his grateful tears, worshipping them and fantasizing over them to achieve his sex orgasm. In ancient China, the Dragon-Gold Pill could provide many Confucians with the psychological comfort. It was a deified sacred object that allowed Confucians to satisfy their ambitions for power.

A Buddhist will shiver with excitement when he touches the Buddha relic. A Christian will shiver with excitement when he touches the Holy Cross. A Muslim will shiver with excitement when he touches the Holy Tomb. The ancient Confucian-bureaucrats also had their own religious emotions. Their god was their emperor. Therefore, when they touched the Dragon-Gold Pill, they also shivered with excitement.

The Dragon-Gold Pill could make Chinese Confucians and bureaucrats strengthen their bodies, live longer, and even live forever. What's wrong with this?

Today, we stand at a new height in history and look at the Dragon-Gold Pill with the perspective of science, civilization, and morality and feel very bored. Yes, eating shit is really boring. But if you look at this thing from the background of ancient China, you will find that the Dragon-Gold Pill was not only a holy thing for Chinese scholars and officials, but also their God's gift. Without it, they had nowhere to live.

So how did the ancient Chinese turn the shit into a fashionable custom? In the next section, I will sketch for you the history and culture of the feces eating by some Chinese people.

Two thousand years ago, after the reunification of China, Confucianism began to dominate Chinese history. The essence of Confucianism is the idea of minions. The two thousand years of Chinese history is the history of training minions. Minion thinking is shit-eating thinking. Chinese dynasties have been historical records of eating shit. In order to please their superiors and to show their loyalty, many lower-level officials took the initiative to rush to taste the shit of the higher-level officials.

The most famous incident of eating shit was during the Spring and Autumn Period and the Warring States Period. As a prisoner of war, King Goujian of the kingdom of Yue, rushed to eat the shit of King Fuchai, of the kingdom of Wu, in order to survive.

Chinese people eat not only shit but also people. Archaeological discoveries show that the Hemudu people in China had the habit of eating children five thousand years ago. Since then, it has never ceased. The Chinese classics of different dynasties have introduced the history and the methods of cannibalism in detail. In the archaeological note, Chicken Ribs, which written by the medical scientist Zhuang Chuo of the Song Dynasty, introduced different ways to eat fat people, thin people, old people, children, babies and embryos. People are not only a delicious dish, but also a very good medicinal material.

This is the traditional Chinese cannibal culture. It's nothing special at all; people usually ate someone if there was nothing else. In the Tang Dynasty, the human meat sold in restaurants was cheaper than the dog meat. In periods of war or famine, the phenomenon of cannibalism was even more tragic. In the ancient Chinese army, when fighting, they often ran out of food, and could only eat the captured-prisoners as food. Many history books recorded that the Chinese are the two-legged sheep. That is, the Chinese are sheep with two legs. The Chinese can be eaten as sheep.

The most famous example is that the rebellious army general Huang Chao in the Tang Dynasty killed all 1,000 captives one day, cooked them, and treated the soldiers to a feast.

The Chinese not only ate people but also drank urine. In Chinese culture, human urine was also called golden water, dragon-phoenix liquid, holy beverage, gold-juice, etc. It had many nicknames. Urine could be good for health and was used for treatment. It was commonly known as urine therapy, or dragon-phoenix liquid therapy.

Urine therapy was created by Laotzi who was the greatest philosopher in China 2,500 years ago and the founder of Chinese Taoism. Later Chinese generations are always worshiping him. According to the Taoist philosophy of the unity of man and nature, nature itself is a manufacturing plant, and every object created by god is beneficial to people, and it can be used endlessly. Therefore, urine is beneficial to people.

The most famous drinking incident is the love story between Zhu Jianshen and Wan Zhen'er. In the Ming Dynasty, Emperor Zhu Jianshen was fed by a royal maiden, Wan Zhen'er, from his childhood. According to Taoism's health-preserving theory, that the masculine and feminine, the positive and the negative, must be mixed, and then the world will be harmony. So she asked him to drink the sweet juice of her physical three peaks. That was, she often rewarded him for drinking her oral saliva, breast lotions, and vaginal secretions. She was more than seventeen years older than him. He listened to her and often drank her urine. Since then, he became a model of the Oedipus complex. He loved her and was intoxicated.

After growing up, he became an emperor and she became his concubine. Even though he had many concubines, she was his favorite. One day, she asked him to kill all his sons in order to be loyal to her. He readily agreed and killed his sons.

At last one day, she had grown old and sick, and she died. He was heartbroken. Without her, he could not survive at all. Then he also died of illness. That love relationship between the old and the young ended here.

This was a disaster caused by drinking urine.

The Chinese not only drank urine but also ate menstruation. There were four major studies in ancient China: astrology, geography, alchemy, and practice. Both alchemy and practice believed that a woman's menstruation was the best gift in the world and could be taken as food. Especially the first menstruations of virgins were the best treasure in the world and should be cherished. Therefore, the traditional setting of the Chinese royal palace was to fill the harem with 10,000 virgins so that the emperor could have fresh menstruation to eat at any time.

In one year, Yang Guang, an emperor of the Sui Dynasty, had widely selected 100,000 virgins into his harem for his enjoyment.

The Renyin Palace Incident was exciting. In 1542, several court ladies who could not provide menstruation to the emperor on the bed were unbearably tortured and anxiously attacked the emperor, so they tried to use a piece of yellow silk to strangle the shameless Emperor Jiajing of the Ming Dynasty. In the end they were defeated, captured, and killed.

Chinese culture is really broad and profound and all-encompassing. Even eating feces, drinking urine, and sipping menstruation, the Chinese could enjoy elegance, respect, and sacredness.

If you think this was a unique phenomenon in ancient China, you are wrong. In modern times, some people are eating shit. After the Great Leap Forward movement in 1958, 75 million Chinese people starved to death. During the period, many hungry farmers secretly followed the commune cadres, scouted when they shitted, and found their shit to eat. Because the hungry people thought that the food of cadres is nutritious, then the feces they excreted would also be rich in nutrients.

In backward rural China, some women secretly ate Buddha's shit one hundred years ago to strengthen their Buddhist beliefs. Buddha's shit was the shit excreted by the monks.

Maybe you will remember a news picture. In recent years, a famine occurred in an African country. A child followed behind a buffalo. When it shitted, he stretched his mouth to its anus to eat the shit. Hunger is really unbearable!

I have one more thing to tell you. Over the past few months, the Wuhan plague has erupted around the world. Do you know how the farmers in Guizhou Province, China, are preventing the epidemic? According to the ancient remedies, they put the buffalo feces into a large pot, added some Chinese herbal medicines, boiled it, and used it as herbal tea, which was distributed to every villager to drink. In history, they used this method to dodge the plague many times.

Herbal medicine does have a curative effect. I was born in Guangdong, and when I was young, whenever I had a cold, I drank Wanglaoji and Qingbaoliang; one is herbal tea, and the other is soup seasoning. Now I live in the United States and drink Coca-Cola every time I have a cold. Coca-Cola has medicinal value. Using it to cook with ginger can cure the cold.

This means that humans have been exploring the use of herbs to cure diseases for thousands of years. Human shit is also explored as a kind of herbal medicine.

Have you heard of cat-shit coffee? This is a top coffee enjoyment. The Indonesian civet-cat eats the coffee fruit, and the coffee pulps are digested in its stomach, but the coffee beans are not digested and are excreted as shit. Kopi Luwak, also known as the cat-shit coffee, is made from this manure. It is described as the most fragrant shit in the world. It is also the most expensive coffee in the world. The raw materials are US$1,000 per kilo. The general market price is $168 for a four-ounce cup.

Cat-shit coffee is found in coffee shops in major cities around the world. There is also a special coffee shop in Macao called Cat-Shit Coffee.

Starting from the invention of cat-shit coffee by Indonesians, nowadays, the Thais have come up with elephant-shit coffee, and the Vietnamese have created cattle-shit coffee. It is nothing more than giving some coffee fruit to elephants and cattle to eat. After the animals' gastrointestinal fermentation, the shits that are excreted will give the coffee beans a different flavor. In this way, customers have a mouthful of enjoyment and will be full of praise.

The civet-cat is kept in a cage and specializes in shit to produce the expensive cat-shit coffee for customers. In Japan, some restaurants specialize in providing actresses who are like the civet-cats. They specialize in shit to produce the expensive human-shit fried dumpling, to supply customers.

Only the Japanese could have raised eating-shit to the level of elegant, exquisite, comfortable, and noble food. In Tokyo, some restaurants specialize in using human excrement to entertain guests. The actresses offered in some restaurants are not allowed to drink alcohol or eat meat a week in advance. They are only allowed to eat vegetables, fruit, rice, and tea, and fasting to keep their stomachs clean. After the diners enter the restaurant, they will accompany an actress to bathe in the hot spring together and then change clothes to maintain the solemnity of the ceremony.

Then the actress will shit in public on the table. The chefs will use a large plate to receive her shit, and add tofu, ham, cod, okra, onion, fennel, black garlic, tomato, corn, leek, peanut oil, MSG, sweet cooking wine, meat and bone powder, grapefruit vinegar, and oyster sauce or shrimp sauce. After stirring, this is poured into a wok and stir-fried; the smell will disappear.

At this time, there is a scented pot with shit in an iron pan. Some customers who like spicy food can also cut some peppers into pellets and add them. Then, with a spoon, they scoop out the shit in the scented pot, put it on pieces of flour crust, and then wrap the flour crust to make them into dumplings. Then, having drizzled peanut oil into the iron pan, the fried dumpling is put in to fry, drizzled with water, and covered. After frying for a while, it will be made the delicious actress fried dumpling.

At the same time, take some squid, bamboo prawn, green pepper, eggplant, lotus root, star eel, mushroom, bean, and radish paste with batter, make it into tempura, and send to the fryer. Then, put the tempura and actress fried dumpling out of the fryer and the pan, and send them to the table. Of course, the shit girl will lie on the desktop. Her body is naked with the fascinating fragrance, which is the ultimate in hospitality, famous around the world: the female body presentation, *nyotaimori*.

So let's have a meal. Accompanied by soy sauce, wasabi, sesame, sliced ginger, shell vinegar, sake and miso soup, and add a plate of lobster sashimi and a plate of Arctic shell sashimi, and also add a plate of Inari sushi. Then, add a plate of Snowflake Fatty Cow made with teppanyaki. Finally, add a bowl of mutton noodle. Just like that, let's call our friends for a cheerful time, and eat the actress shit together. That is really wonderful!

This kind of food enjoys a special cultural atmosphere. It is to satisfy the ultimate fantasies of those erotic fans in the world. Life is alive, to be able to worship a goddess in such a way, and even eat her shit with relish—how much joy and satisfaction that would be!

This is why I am determined to overthrow the Trump Dynasty! President Trump's worship of the Chinese emperor Xi Jinping has reached the level of obsession and madness. Every lie of Chairman Xi Jinping is regarded as God's truth by President Trump. Even if Xi Jinping excretes a pile of shit, Trump cannot help eating it. I must give President Trump the nickname "Shit-Eating Emperor" so that when he decides to become emperor in 2025, my book *How to Destroy America* can become a time bomb to explode, and the Trump Dynasty can vanish in the explosion.

This letter I have written to you will appear in *How to Destroy America*. This book is a powerful ideological weapon. I hope that every member of the United States Congress will read this book in the next few years and learn to use this ideological weapon: Shishengism.

In addition, I advise you do not need to treat the enemy with mercy as would Mother Teresa. President Trump is not only a national enemy, but also a global enemy! Today, you may think that I have criticized and vilified President Trump in this way too much. But you must foresee the severity of President Trump's damage to all humankind and to the United States. Thousands upon thousands of people have become perished, thousands upon thousands more have committed suicide in despair, thousands upon thousands of families have been destroyed, and thousands upon thousands of people have lost their loved ones. All the dead people can't find a reasonable method of revenge. Only my book *How to Destroy America*, by flogging and trampling President Trump, can give them a little comfort.

May God bless you!

May 30, 2020
Washington, DC

Postscript

My postscript is a quotation from Ms. Sheng Xue:

Fascism, communism, and terrorism are the three malignant tumors in the history of human social development. Fascism has basically passed, but we still face a very serious situation ….

The fundamentalist terrorism led by paranoid ultra-Muslims and the materialistic CCP's state terrorism are deeply affecting the humanistic environment and the value orientation of the entire world and are likely to destroy the world's civilization and order.

The former absolutely belongs to the spiritual realm, and the latter completely belongs to the material. The former believes that it is on the road to the truth, and the latter believes that the truth can be replaced by power. The former must kill the dissidents to clear the way to the realm of truth, and the latter must kill the dissidents to guarantee the possession of power. The former uses the wonderful paradise transformed by the pure spirit to attract the souls who are tired of the world, and the latter uses the luxury of powerful materials to fascinate the dying bodies.

When the free will of the civilized world cannot stop the neat and shocking pace of radical terrorism, and when the universal values of the democratic countries cannot withstand the assault of the CCP's soft and hard force and its powerful material desires, these two antihuman rebellious civilizations will merge together.

When these two extreme evil powers meet, the world will be destroyed.

Therefore, doing our utmost to end the CCP's tyranny as quickly as possible is the Chinese people's greatest contribution to the world for democracy and peace.

The above is a short essay published by Ms. Sheng Xue on her Facebook page in the spring of 2020. The appendix is a picture of a gathering of Nazi Germany she published on Facebook.

In order to demonstrate power, during the Second World War, Adolf Hitler, the great German dictator, always liked to organize large gatherings to show his will as a ruler and to train the people.

Sheng Xue is very smart. She is a great thinker. She wrote the above short essay with her wisdom as a historical prophet.

I used her short essay as a postscript to my book, just to give the world a piece of evidence that her political thought has covered the academic scholars for the next thousand years.

And *How to Destroy America*? This book is essentially a key to opening the door to China's democratic palace. How to overthrow the CCP? This book has explained all the answers. All the action methods and all the action steps have been made clear.

As a result, Shishengism's doctrine has also deduced three new contents: First, the Xi Dynasty cannot be overthrown without overthrowing the Trump Dynasty. Second, China's prodemocracy fighters are the cannon fodder of the American people and the vanguards of the death squad to defend the democratic system of the United States. Third, if the US government does not help the Chinese achieve democracy, the United States and the American people will suffer the damage.

In other words, in order to expand the communist power, the CCP must oppress, crush, and destroy the United States. The United States is a stumbling block to the expansion of the CCP. The United States must either rebel or die. It must choose one of the two. Therefore, China's democracy will be done automatically. As the years go by, the United States must always resist the global expansion of communism.

June 19, 2020
Washington, DC